Gender
and Close
Relationships

SAGE SERIES ON
CLOSE RELATIONSHIPS

Series Editors
Clyde Hendrick, Ph.D., and
Susan S. Hendrick, Ph.D.

Gender and Close Relationships

Barbara A. Winstead
Valerian J. Derlega
Suzanna Rose

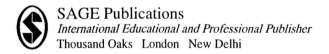

Sage
Series
on Close
Relationships

SAGE Publications
International Educational and Professional Publisher
Thousand Oaks   London   New Delhi

For information:

SAGE Publications, Inc.
2455 Teller Road
Thousand Oaks, California 91320
E-mail: order@sagepub.com

SAGE Publications Ltd.
6 Bonhill Street
London EC2A 4PU
United Kingdom

SAGE Publications India Pvt. Ltd.
M-32 Market
Greater Kailash I
New Delhi 110 048 India

Printed in the United States of America

Library of Congress Cataloging-in-Publication Data

Winstead, Barbara A.
    Gender and close relationships/Barbara A. Winstead, Valerian J. Derlega, Suzanna Rose.
        p. cm.—(Sage series on close relationships)
    Includes bibliographical references (p.) and index.
    ISBN 0-8039-7166-4 (cloth: acid-free paper).—ISBN 0-8039-7167-2 (pbk.: acid-free paper)
    1. Interpersonal relations. 2. Man-woman relationships. 3. Sex differences (Psychology). 4. Women—Psychology. 5. Men—Psychology. I. Derlega, Valerian J. II. Rose, Suzanna. III. Title. IV. Series.
    HM132.W56 1997   96-5126
    306.7—dc21

    97 98 99 00 01 02 03   10 9 8 7 6 5 4 3 2 1

Acquiring Editor:	C. Terry Hendrix
Editorial Assistant:	Dale Mary Grenfell
Production Editor:	Michele Lingre
Production Assistant:	Denise Santoyo
Typesetter/Designer:	Marion S. Warren
Indexer:	Cristina Haley
Cover Designer:	Candice Harman
Print Buyer:	Anna Chin

Contents

Dedicated to Cecilia Wernicki

Series Editors' Introduction

When we first began our work on love attitudes more than a decade ago, we did not know what to call our research area. In some ways it represented an extension of earlier work in interpersonal attraction. Most of our scholarly models were psychologists (although sociologists had long been deeply involved in the areas of courtship and marriage), yet we sometimes felt as if our work had no professional "home". That has all changed. Our research not only has a home but also has an extended family, and the family is composed of relationship researchers. During the past decade, the discipline of close relationships (also called personal relationships and intimate relationships) has emerged, developed, and flourished.

Two aspects of close relationships research should be noted. The first is its rapid growth, resulting in numerous books, journals, handbooks, book series, and professional organizations. As fast as the field grows, the demand for even more research and knowledge seems to be ever increasing. Questions about close personal relationships still far exceed answers. The second noteworthy aspect of the new discipline of close relationships is its interdisciplinary nature. The field owes its vitality to scholars from communications, family studies and human development, psychology (clinical, counseling, developmental, social), and sociology, as well as other disciplines such as nursing and social work. It is this interdisciplinary wellspring that gives close relationships research its diversity and richness, qualities that we hope to achieve in the current series.

The Sage Series on Close Relationships is designed to acquaint diverse readers with the most up-to-date information about various topics in close relationships theory and research. Each volume in the series covers a particular topic or theme in one area of close relationships. Each book reviews the particular topic area, describes contemporary research in the area (including the authors' own work, where appropriate), and offers some suggestions for interesting research questions and/or real-world applications related to the topic. The volumes are designed to be appropriate for students and professionals in communication, family studies, psychology, sociology, and social work, among others. A basic assumption of the series is that the broad panorama of close relationships can best be portrayed by authors from multiple disciplines, so that the series cannot be "captured" by any single disciplinary bias.

We are born into a gendered world, and gender affects virtually all of our close relationships, whether with romantic partners, friends, family members—parents, children, siblings—or work colleagues. Recognizing the fundamental importance of gender and placing it solidly in a scholarly context, Barbara A. Winstead, Valerian J. Derlega, and Suzanna Rose have written a very important book. *Gender and Close Relationships* offers a timely and comprehensive view of the ways in which gender influences (and is sometimes influenced by) our most intimate relationships. As they address topics such as attraction and dating, sexual relations, relationship maintenance, conflict and violence, and friendship, the authors ground the latest social science research on gender firmly in relevant theory. The result is a highly readable, interesting, scholarly, yet practical book about gender and its role in our lives. Working in an area that is volatile and sometimes divisive, Winstead, Derlega, and Rose help us to better understand the current world of gendered interaction as well as to envision a more hopeful future.

CLYDE HENDRICK
SUSAN S. HENDRICK
SERIES EDITORS

Preface

The present book focuses on how *gender* (being a woman or a man or others' reactions to us as a woman or a man) influences what happens in our close relationships. At every stage of a relationship, whether it is initial attraction, getting to know someone, keeping a relationship going, coping with conflict or relationship problems, or facing the loss of a partner, gender affects how individuals interact with one another.

There is considerable discussion in psychology, communications, sociology, and family studies about how much women's and men's behavior is "caused" by nature (inborn characteristics of individuals) and/or nurture (how women's and men's behaviors may be shaped by social expectations and beliefs that operate as externally imposed social norms or as internalized values, attitudes, scripts, and social skills). Besides documenting the importance of gender on individuals' and couples' behaviors in relationships, we will review theory and research on these various gender-linked explanations for what happens in close relationships. Through our examination of different types of relationships and relationship issues (attraction, dating, sexuality, maintenance, conflict and violence, and friendship), we hope to provide you with a better understanding of how gender influences your relationships. Although much research focuses on the impact of gender in heterosexual relationships, there is a burgeoning literature on gender and relationships among gay male and lesbian couples which we also examine.

In preparing this book, we want to extend our thanks to the many individuals who provided assistance. We are grateful to the authors and publishers who gave us permission to use their copyrighted materials, and we thank the many researchers who sent us reprints of their work as we prepared various chapters. We appreciated the patience and support of Susan Hendrick and Clyde Hendrick, who are the editors of the Sage Series on Close Relationships. At Sage, we thank Terry Hendrix and Dale Mary Grenfell for their support of this project. John Derlega wrote the commentary in Chapter 2 on the joys and pitfalls of dating. Jenny Caja provided terrific assistance in editing and typing chapter drafts. The staff in the Graphics Department at Old Dominion University, Susan Cooke, Donald Emminger, and Deborah Miller, gave invaluable support. Barbara Winstead and Valerian Derlega also want to thank Ann and Christopher Winstead-Derlega and Cinnamon the Cat, who enriched our lives during the writing of this book.

1

Introduction

K aren meets Jim at a dorm party. He isn't the best-looking guy
in the room, but when they talk, she can tell he is a serious
student, and he seems to know what he wants to do with his life.
Jim is impressed with Karen, too, but he wonders if gorgeous Gail,
standing across the room, would go out with him. *Are women and
men attracted to different qualities in potential partners? If so, how can
we explain their preferences?*

Karen and Jim have been dating for 6 months. At a party they
have an argument. Karen leaves. Jim stays, drinks, flirts with Gail,
whom he has not seen for several months, and ends up in bed with
her. Karen finds out and is furious. *Do men and women have different
attitudes toward sex? Do they behave differently? How do they feel about
sexual infidelity?*

Ten years later, Karen and Jim are married. Both are school-
teachers. Their children are 4 and 2 years old. *How do they manage*

marriage, parenthood, and careers? Do they share homemaking and child care responsibilities? How do these multiple roles and their division of labor affect Karen's and Jim's happiness and marital satisfaction?

Karen and Jim get together on weekends with their friends Connie and Mark. Karen and Connie get into a conversation about their children. Jim and Mark watch a playoff game and discuss the upcoming Super Bowl. *Are there gender differences in same-sex friendships? If so, how do we understand them?*

From the moment we are born, each of us is identified as female or male. The first thing parents, family, and friends want to know about a healthy baby is: Is it a boy or a girl? These days, many parents know even before birth whether they will have a son or a daughter. What impact does that information have on parents, siblings, or other relatives and friends? In what ways do they prepare themselves for forming a relationship with this new person? Does gender matter? Studies show that perceptions and expectations of infants and children are influenced by the sex of the child (Antill, 1987; Rubin, Provenzano, & Luria, 1974). It is easy to imagine how our image of a child, what she or he looks like, what she or he will be like, what she or he will do when she or he grows up will be affected by attaching that label: girl or boy. This book is in part about the ways in which gender influences how others perceive and treat us.

It is also about how we form relationships and how being female or male may or may not make a difference in the quantity, quality, or content of the relationships we have. Being female or male may influence how we feel about relationships, how we start them or stop them, how we behave while we are in them.

Although focusing on gender, we need to maintain a double vision. Being female or male creates our relationship experiences both by how it stimulates others to behave toward us and by how it influences our own behavior toward others. For example, if Pat believes that women are kinder and more understanding than men, Pat will share personal information with Mary but not John regardless of whether Mary—or John—wants to hear it. Mary is the recipient of relationship-enhancing behavior from Pat whether she wants to be or not. This is how being a woman or a man can affect how we are treated by others. Data suggest that women, on average, are more responsive listeners than men. So Mary might know more about a lot of people than John does because *she* is a better listener than *he* is. In this way, gender affects how women and men behave in relationships. Throughout the book, we will try to keep both of these avenues of influence in mind.

The connection between individual and relationship is also circular. We seek relationships and shape them; we are also changed by them. Most people acknowledge that their parents influenced them when they were young, but good and bad relationships later in life can also alter who we are.

ઑ Explaining Gender Differences in Relationships

Most of the research presented in this text will include subject's sex (that is, whether a research participant is female or male) or stimulus person's sex (i.e., whether the person being responded to is female or male) as a major category of analysis. Gender differences that emerge from these analyses are often fascinating; but they cannot tell us *why* females and males are different. If we read that males have more positive attitudes toward casual sex than females do and report having more sexual partners than females do, we may be ready to say, "Well, that's because. . . ." —you fill in the blank. Maybe you think it has to do with male levels of testosterone (a biological explanation); or you may think it has to do with the double standard, "good girls don't" (a socialization explanation); or maybe you think it is just reporting bias, that is, males will tell you that they approve of casual sex and have many sexual partners and females won't tell you that, but if you could actually *know* what they do or how they really feel, you would find no gender difference at all. Whatever you think *causes* these gender differences, the fact is that a study surveying females and males and reporting these differences tells us nothing at all about what causes these differences to occur. It takes studies that actually examine potential causal factors to answer questions about why, and often even those studies have their limitations. For example, to test whether the cause of certain differences really is testosterone or socialization, we would, as researchers, have to control levels of testosterone and socialization experiences (e.g., how research participants are treated by parents, teachers) over the lifetime of the participants and then see if different levels of testosterone or different treatment by others affected attitudes toward casual sex or number of partners. Not only would this be extremely difficult to do, it would also be unethical.

Debates about causes of gender differences will continue, and data that can help us resolve these debates will generally be limited. It is not, however, necessary to think of sex as a purely biological or purely social variable. When psychologists pose a question of either/or, the best answer is usually both.

Currently, several explanations have been proposed to account for gender differences in relationships. These explanations can be described in terms of two dimensions: structural versus individual and socialization versus biology. (See Figure 1.1.)

Structural refers to the ways in which current roles (e.g., being a husband, being a mother), situations, and/or the expectations of others shape our behavior. The other end of this dimension is *individual,* referring to the assumption that our behavior is governed by our personal traits and characteristics. The second dimension, socialization versus biology, works on the assumption that the explanation of behavior is individual, but that individual differences may be acquired in different ways, either through learning and socialization or through the effects of biological processes, such as hormones.

✒ Dimension 1: Structural Versus Individual

If you are chosen by a group to be its leader, your behavior in that group is affected by your role as leader. If someone asks you to help, you become a helpful person. In these examples, your being a leader or being helpful is not so much caused by your individual characteristics as by the role you are given and the expectations of others. The idea that your behavior is determined by outside forces, social expectations and constraints, and situational demands is the *structural* approach. Others would argue

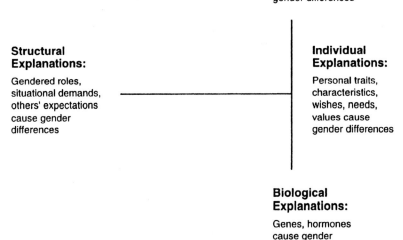

Figure 1.1. Explanations for Gender Differences in Relationships Described Along Two Dimensions: Structural Versus Individual and Socialization Versus Biology

that you become a leader because you have the abilities, motives, and so on, that make you a leader, or that you are asked to help because you are, by your nature, a helpful person. This individual approach tends to ignore the influences of opportunity (or lack of opportunity) to be a leader or to be helpful. The next sections will describe examples of the structural and individual approaches to explaining gender differences.

Structural Explanations. Eagly (1987) has presented a social role interpretation of gender differences in social behavior. She argues that the major source of role differences for women and men is the division of labor between the sexes: Women occupy communal roles, such as caretaker, homemaker, service provider; men occupy agentic or instrumental roles, such as breadwinner, manager, head of household. There is also a status difference between women's and men's roles, with men occupying the higher status and the more powerful roles. Division of labor between the sexes affects gender differences in social behavior in two ways: (1) It leads to gender-role expectations, and (2) it leads to sex-typed skills and beliefs (Eagly, 1987, p. 32). Eagly and Steffen (1984) found that perceptions of others in terms of communal and agentic attributes are influenced by the occupations they have, regardless of their sex, and Eagly and Wood (1982) documented that higher status persons are seen as influential and lower status persons as influenceable, again regardless of the sex of the person. So the fact that women are observed primarily in certain roles (mother, teacher, nurse, secretary) and men in others (manager, president, technician) does affect expectations about women's and men's characteristic social behaviors.

These expectations, in turn, have been found to influence behavior. In a study of the self-perpetuating nature of stereotypes about women and men, Skrypnek and Snyder (1982) had men interact with a female partner (without actually meeting), but in half of the pairs, the male believed his partner was another male. The members of each pair had to agree on who would do each of a list of 24 tasks. Females interacting with a male who *believed* his partner was a male tended to choose more masculine tasks than females interacting with a male who *believed* his partner was female. In other words, the male's belief about the sex of partner influenced the partner's behavior such that the partner tended to confirm the male's belief. Psychologists call this the self-fulfilling prophecy.

According to Eagly (1987), the second way roles affect social behavior is by influencing the skills that individuals develop and their beliefs about themselves. Parents typically assign different chores to their female and male children. If girls are expected to baby-sit younger siblings more often than boys, they will develop caretaking skills. If boys are asked to help with car or house repair, they will acquire mechanical skills. Learning skills by being in different roles is a lifelong process, but it also affects us as adults in our ongoing interactions with others. As suggested earlier, if you are chosen to be the leader of a group, you will probably try to act like a leader. If you find you do not have all the skills you need to be a good leader, you will probably try to learn them quickly.

An approach similar to Eagly's is microstructural theory. Like Eagly, Risman and Schwartz (1989) question the assumption "that gender is internalized as a stable personality trait" (p. 3). They argue, that "taken to its logical extreme, our microstructural theory predicts that men and women would behave *exactly* the same way if they were given identical expectations and positions in society" (p. 3). They acknowledge that women and men enter interactions and roles with biological and socialization histories, but they emphasize that *current* opportunities and constraints may shape behavior more than individualistic factors. To examine this theory, Risman (1987) studied men who were single fathers and compared them with single mothers and mothers and fathers in dual-earner and traditional families. She asked: Is it the role of primary caretaker or is it gender that determines caretaking behavior? As with most research, the findings are complex. Parental role had a strong impact on housework, especially for men. Single fathers reported a much higher level of responsibility for household work than fathers in other situations. For expressions of overt affection, men and women who shared responsibility for child care reported higher levels than either women or men who were single parents or traditional fathers. Still, women reported being more physically affectionate than men did. The best predictor of parent-child intimacy was feminine personality traits, but somewhat surprisingly, although men had lower scores on femininity than women, single fathers had higher scores than other men and scores almost identical to mothers in dual-earner couples. Single mothers and traditional mothers had higher scores than dual-earner mothers. So, what we generally consider to be a personality trait, femininity, predicts parent-child intimacy, but this trait is in turn predicted by one's parenting role. In sum, the data suggest that men who are in the role of "mother" (i.e., primary caretaker) acquire the characteristics necessary to do the job.

These two theories, role theory and microstructural theory, emphasize the importance of current opportunities and constraints in determining gender differences in relationship behaviors. If men are chosen to be leaders, men will be more authoritative than women. If women are chosen to take notes at the meeting, women will be more attentive listeners than men.

Individual Explanations. Other explanations assume gender differences are the result of the individual's personal motives, personality traits, biologically determined tendencies, or other characteristics that "belong" to the individual and not to the situation or role the individual is in. These explanations assume that women and men would *not* respond the same way to the same situational demands but would respond differently because as females and males, they have fundamentally different needs, wishes, and personalities. These explanations range, however, from those that argue that these differences arise from women and men having a different set of experiences, starting in infancy, to those that argue that biological differences between females and males inevitably lead to gender differences in personality and social behavior.

⁀ Dimension 2: Socialization Versus Biology

Socialization refers to the ways in which family, society, and culture affect the development of individual characteristics. *Biology* refers to the genetic and/or physiological factors that may influence individual traits.

Socialization Explanations. The general ideas behind socialization explanations are, perhaps, the easiest to grasp. Essentially, this explanation says that we are taught in various ways how to be females and males and that having learned, we are henceforth different. It is the "how we learn" part that distinguishes among socialization theories. Whiting and Edwards, who are social anthropologists, based on their observations of children in diverse cultures, conclude that gender differences in nurturance (females greater) and dominance (males greater) are the result of the different amounts of time that girls and boys spend interacting with different social partners (Whiting & Edwards, 1988). In most cultures, children 6 to 10 years of age act as child nurses to younger children. Girls are more likely to be assigned this task than boys. Very young children elicit caretaking responses from others, and if adequate caretaking is not forthcoming, they cry and complain, effectively shaping caretakers to become more skilled in their nurturing abilities. Whiting and Edwards (1988) argue that by being in the role of child nurse more frequently than males, females acquire nurturing characteristics. Boys, on the other hand, are more likely than girls to interact with peers. In their observations, dominance conflicts are frequent between peers, and children learn to be competitive in these interactions. This approach is similar to the role and microstructural theories discussed above; only now it is argued that by repetitively playing certain roles in childhood, females and males develop different personal characteristics.

Bem (1993) describes the socialization process as a learning of schemas or the acquisition of lenses through which we see the world and ourselves. These lenses are gender polarization and androcentricism. Gender polarization refers to the emphasis placed on gender differences, the belief that females and males are fundamentally different and that anyone who deviates from their appropriate gender role is not all right. Bem cites many examples of the imposition of this belief, starting with the color coding of infants (girls = pink; boys = blue). The point is that children learn not only how to be a girl or a boy but also that girls and boys *are different*. This schema is also applied to the self. We each check to see that who we are and how we behave fits the culture's rules for being female or male, knowing that if we don't fit, then we might be perceived to be the "opposite" sex or too much like the other sex. There are social penalties for being too masculine if you are female, and especially for being feminine if you are male.

Much of Bem's research has focused on individual differences in gender schematicity (the degree to which each of us has acquired the gender polarization lens and applies it to ourselves). She has shown that conventionally gendered people (females describing themselves as feminine and males describing themselves as masculine) are more likely to avoid gender-inappropriate tasks (Bem & Lenney, 1976), more likely to confuse female speakers with other females and male speakers with other males (Frable & Bem, 1985), and more likely to cluster words according to their femininity or masculinity (Bem, 1981) than were nonconventionally gendered individuals. Frable (1989) also found that conventionally gendered individuals were more likely than others to accept gender rules about behavior (e.g., females, but not males, can wear nail polish and cry; males, but not females, can order dinner in a restaurant and engage in and enjoy casual sex). Males were also more likely to pay attention to the sex of job applicants for a management trainee position and to denigrate the female job applicant's interview and, for males only, to endorse sexist language.

The second lens that Bem (1993) describes is androcentricism, which is the assumption that male is normal and better than female. The classic example from psychology is Freudian theory, in which Freud asserts that all children, girls included, want a penis and are concerned about losing it (or having already lost it!). But there are many additional examples from religion, law, and psychological research demonstrating our assumption that the way men are is normal and that women are not quite normal or at least different from men in fundamental ways. An example from the literature on adult roles and their effect on mental health will give you an idea of what Bem means by androcentricism. Most people, including psychologists, assume that proper roles for adults include (1) having a relationship partner (marriage); (2) parenthood; and (3) work. Not every adult, female or male, actually does all of these things, but most do. For men, these three roles (e.g., husband, father, worker) form an image of the mature, successful male. But for women, psychologists saw a different picture. Wouldn't a woman who tried to be a wife, mother, and worker experience role conflict or role strain? Given the responsibility that women are generally given for maintaining relationship, home, and children, the assumption that work outside the home would be a stressful extra burden for her is perhaps understandable. But when psychologists actually did the research on women's multiple roles, they found repeatedly that women who work outside the home, even women with committed relationships and children, are happier and less depressed than women without all of these roles to play (Crosby, 1991; Warr & Parry, 1982). In this case, the assumption that women would be different from men, or perhaps that women couldn't handle something that men can, was not borne out by the research. There are rewards from each of the roles that adults play, and both women and men benefit from those rewards.

These lenses of gender polarization and androcentricism are imposed on us from birth and are learned from many sources. They also, like social roles, affect who we are and how we behave at any given moment.

Other socialization theories assume that development of gender differences occurs not just cumulatively and continuously, but also early in life. Chodorow (1978), using object relations theory as a foundation, concludes that "girls and boys develop different relational capacities and senses of self as a result of growing up in a family in which women mother" (p. 173). An infant's earliest identifications are with her or his primary caretaker. When this primary caretaker is female (i.e., a mother), two things happen: (1) the female caretaker identifies with a daughter in a different way than she does with a son and, (2) the daughter's identifications with the caretaker are continuous, whereas a son's will shift to a same-sex other. The mutual identification between mother and daughter accounts for the daughters developing a capacity for empathy and relationship. A woman first learns to be attuned to others in this close relationship with her mother. A son is seen by the mother as different, and so a basis for his separateness and capacity to form an independent identity and autonomy are established. Chodorow does not argue that mothers care more or better for female than male children, but that mothers identify with daughters more than with sons because daughters are the same sex. Think of a child you have or might have some day. Try to imagine in detail what that child's life is like and will be like in the future. Try to imagine what the child's inner experiences are like. You will probably have an easier time if the child is the same sex as you. The sense of understanding what it is like or will be like for a same-sex child is greater because you share similar bodies and similar experiences. Of course, the child may have very different feelings and experiences that you are not aware of, but the sense of identification remains. According to Chodorow, the connectedness between mother and daughter and separateness between mother and son are established very early in the child's life and result in gender differences in personality and social relationships.

There are other approaches to understanding gender socialization, but these serve as examples. What socialization theories share is the assumption that if societies changed, so would gender differences. If, for example, girls and boys were assigned to the same roles and spent the same amount of time interacting with smaller children, peers, and adults, they would not develop different interpersonal skills and interests. If society did not emphasize gender differences, children would not concentrate on learning the rules that allow us to tell female from male and apply those rules to themselves and others. And if men were primary caretakers, males would be the more empathic and nurturing gender and females would be the more autonomous and independent; or perhaps if women and men shared caretaking, these characteristics would also be shared equally.

Biological Explanations. When we think of biological differences between females and males, we think of genes and hormones. Females have two X chromosomes; males have an X and a Y. Females have more estrogen and progesterone, and males have more testosterone. But direct links in humans between genes or hormones and behavior are often not impressive and/or replicable. Furthermore, the moment we are born and come under the influence of our environment, the direction of causation between biology and behavior becomes complex. Situations and behaviors affect physiological processes just as physiological processes affect behavior.

There is research, however, that considers the effects of prenatal hormones on subsequent behavior. It is research on girls born with adrenogenital syndrome (AGS), also called congenital adrenal hyperplasia (CAH). This is a family of disorders (occurring in 1 in 5,000-15,000 newborns) associated with errors in metabolism resulting in greater production of sex steroids during fetal development and, in females, in varying degrees of masculinization of the genitalia. Studies of females with these disorders, who have been surgically corrected and hormonally treated from birth, have focused on what impact the presence of "masculinizing" hormones during fetal development has on the personality and social behavior of these girls. Ehrhardt summarizes her research by stating that the AGS/CAH girls differ from controls in

> (i) a combination of intense outdoor play, increased association with male peers, long-term identification as a "tomboy" by self and others, probably all related to high energy expenditure, and (ii) decreased parenting rehearsal such as doll play and baby care, and a low interest in the role rehearsal of wife and mother versus having a career. (Ehrhardt & Meyer-Bahlburg, 1981, p. 1314)

In a recent study conducted in Germany, 35 patients with AGS/CAH were compared to healthy sisters, using self and mother assessments (Dittman et al., 1990). These researchers found no differences in high-energy expenditure or in social behaviors, such as dominance, assertiveness, or acceptance by peers. AGS/CAH females did however, express less of a "wish for own children" and a greater "preference for career vs. family." The AGS/CAH females also rated themselves and were rated by their mothers as less interested in their appearance and in female-typical play. The presence of androgens during fetal development in the girls with AGS/CAH may cause these more masculine/less feminine behaviors.

Reviewers of these studies have pointed out that these individuals are experiencing a chronic illness for which they receive surgery and hormonal treatment (Hines, 1982). Many of these girls are born with a penis and empty scrotum. Their parents, although assured they will be corrected hormonally and anatomically, may nevertheless wonder about the gender status of their child and her future as a woman. Also, as illustrated above, although some evidence of psychological masculinization is found in most studies, the specific findings vary from study to study.

Evolutionary Theory. The most influential current biologically based theory of gender and relationships is evolutionary psychology. Evolutionary psychology derives predictions of and explanations for behavior from evolutionary theory. According to Buss (1991), the aim of this "new discipline . . . is to identify psychological mechanisms and behavioral strategies as evolved solutions to the adaptive problems our species has faced over millions of years" (pp. 459-460). For some gender differences, Buss proposes that females and males are genetically predisposed to behave in different ways.

The evolutionary explanation for gender differences rests on two foundations: sexual selection and parental investment. The theory of sexual selection states that individuals compete with same-sex others for reproductively valuable partners; that males will be more variable than females in their reproductive success; that female and male mate preferences will differ; and that these preferences will influence what competition between same-sex individuals is all about. Trivers's (1972) theory of parental investment is an elaboration of the theory of sexual selection. It states that females invest more time and energy in offspring (pregnancy, lactation) and have fewer opportunities to contribute genetically to offspring than males (each pregnancy and period of lactation generally preclude new pregnancies). Males, on the other hand, can invest as little as one ejaculation and can contribute genetically, theoretically, to countless offspring. Thus, according to these authors, mate preferences, mating strategies, and relationship behaviors will show predictable gender differences, such as: Females prefer mates who have earning capacity, social status, and dominance, whereas males prefer mates who are physically attractive (Buss, 1989). Buss (1988) also finds that males, more than females, report using resource display (e.g., spending money, driving a nice car) to attract heterosexual partners; and females, more than males, report enhancing physical appearance to attract heterosexual partners. These gender differences are interpreted in terms of females wanting or needing mates who can provide resources for themselves and their offspring, and males wanting or needing mates who are healthy and fertile (indicated by physical attractiveness). The association of females with relationship-oriented behaviors and males with competitive behaviors is also explained in terms of sex-differentiated strategies for reproductive success. Females must nurture their limited number of offspring, whereas males must compete with other males to have resources to be attractive to women and to provide for their offspring.

Despite the assumption of evolutionary psychology that these gender differences are genetically predisposed, some researchers using an evolutionary approach also consider sociocultural factors that influence reproductive strategies. For example, fewer sex differences in reproductive behaviors are expected and found in monogamous (one partner per person) societies than in polygynous (more than one wife per husband) societies. Furthermore, Lancaster (1989) argues that when women can command resources and men have unpredictable or inadequate resources, women tend to form households that exclude men and a woman may even enhance her reproductive success by having children by more than one man to increase her access to male resources. Draper and Belsky (1990) suggest that the father's presence or absence can predict an offspring's onset of puberty, sexual behavior, and relationship stability (preparing them for reproductive success via monogamous [father present] or nonmonogamous [father absent] relationships).

In recent years, researchers using the evolutionary psychology approach have focused particularly on gender differences in relationships and sexuality. Many of these studies will be discussed in subsequent chapters.

Although this two-dimensional scheme is useful for understanding the different approaches to explaining gender differences, always remember that we do not have to choose one single approach in trying to explain gender differences. In fact, each of the approaches described above helps us in understanding the complexities of gender and relationships.

ᴈ Preview

As you read this book, you will see that we refer back to the various theories we have just discussed. None can be proved or disproved. Each can be used as a way of explaining gender differences in relationships. In the last chapter of the book, we will revisit these theories and assess them in light of all we have learned about gender and relationships.

Each of the subsequent chapters takes up an important aspect of relationships. Chapter 2 deals with attraction and dating, that is, how relationships get started. Are women and men interested in the same or different types of partners? If there are gender differences, what are they and why might they occur? When women and men begin to date, what rules or "scripts" do they follow? What happens to gender differences found in heterosexual relationships when we look at romantic attraction and dating in same-sex couples?

Once a relationship has been established, and sometimes even before, couples grapple with the issue of sexuality. Do women and men have different attitudes toward and experiences with sex? Chapter 3 explores the issue of gender and sexuality. Relationships start and end, often accompanied by strong feelings on the part of relationships partners. But most relationships at any given moment are in a maintenance phase, neither beginning nor ending, but just "going on." Chapter 4 considers gender and relationship maintenance. Do women do more than men to keep and maintain relationships, as one often hears? What contributes to relationship satisfaction for women and men? What sorts of "work" do relationships require, and who does it?

Relationships do not always run smoothly. Every relationship is visited by conflict. How do men and women deal with conflict? Why is it that 16% to 35% of couples will experience physical violence in their relationship this year? Chapter 5 deals with conflict and abuse in heterosexual and homosexual relationships.

Chapters 2 through 5 explore the ups and downs of romantic relationships and how they are affected by gender. Chapter 6 is about friendships. Although we may spend more emotional time and energy on our romantic relationships (and we devote more pages to them in this book), friendships are often the relationships that sustain us. Do women and men form similar or different same-sex friendships? And, what about cross-sex friendships? Chapter 7 considers general patterns presented in the preceding chapters and connects them with theories presented in the first chapter. We will also make some suggestions about questions that need to be asked by relationship researchers. Last but not least, we will present questions that you might ask yourself about your relationships and how you feel about the interplay of gender and relationships in your own life.

2

Attraction and Dating

Jay, a junior at a midwestern American university, is attending a party at a friend's house during spring break. Jay tells someone he just met, Meg, that he wanted to go to Florida over spring break, but the trip fell through because he could not take off from his job. Meg stares icily at Jay and says she does not understand why anyone would want to go to a place where there would be so many people hanging out. Jay, feeling rejected by Meg's response, wanders off to refill his drink. He walks over (although a bit hesitantly) to where Brenda is standing. Jay introduces himself and mentions that he has been working during spring break. Brenda, in turn, says how she has been juggling a part-time job and doing library research for a term paper during the break, even though she would have liked to have gotten away. Jay perks up and mentions how he had wanted to go to Florida but it didn't work out. Jay and Brenda spend a lot of time talking together that evening. Before the party is over Jay invites Brenda to go out to dinner with him the next evening.

Nearly everyone has at least one romantic partner in life. Most of us have more than one; some of us have many. Among all the people we meet and interact with, who do we find attractive, who do we seek to get to know better, and how do we go about it? When individuals start a relationship, they make many decisions, including how interested they are in the other person and how to present themselves to the other person (in terms of what they say and how they act). They also make decisions about whether to "speed up" or "slow down" the pace of the development of the relationship. In this chapter, we will discuss how gender influences *who* individuals are attracted to and *how* they behave in developing relationships.

➤ Choice of a Romantic Partner

Let's imagine that we are looking for someone for a long-term or committed relationship. Read the following list of characteristics and rank them for their importance or desirability in a partner. First, give a 1 to the most important characteristic, a 2 to the second most important characteristic, and so forth, until you assign a 13 to the lowest ranked characteristic in a potential partner. The characteristics are (see Buss & Barnes, 1986, p. 567):

5	kind and understanding 1	13 wants children 10
3	religious 2	6 easygoing 9
	exciting personality 7	12 good heredity 12
9	creative and artistic 11	7 college graduate 5
10	good housekeeper 6	4 physically attractive 4
1	intelligent 3	healthy 8
11	good earning capacity 13	

In a study conducted by Buss and Barnes (1986), male and female undergraduate students were asked to rank order the desirability of these characteristics in someone they might marry. The males and females agreed that the most important characteristics in a marriage partner were kind and understanding, exciting personality, and intelligent. They also agreed that the least important characteristics were good heredity, good housekeeper, and religious. However, there were sex differences in the importance given to three characteristics that might be found in a potential mate. "Physically attractive" was rated higher in importance by males than females, and "good earning" capacity and "college graduate" were rated higher in importance by females than males.

The results of Buss and Barnes's (1986) study indicate that women and men hold similar and dissimilar opinions about what characteristics should be sought in a mate. There are, of course, obvious advantages for both sexes to selecting a partner who is smart, interesting, and easy to get along with. But there may also be greater advantages to one sex than the other to selecting certain characteristics in a mate. According to the evolutionary model of mate selection (see Chapter 1), women invest more time and energy than men in having and raising children. Because females have less potential for producing offspring than men and they are likely to invest more in nurturing their children, females may be more likely to value characteristics in a partner that are associated with economic success. The material resources and social status that such a man has will be an advantage to the woman's offspring. The greater investment that women make in raising children may explain why females, compared to males, prefer to marry someone who has good earning capacity and who is a college graduate.

According to the evolutionary argument, males are assumed to increase their reproductive success by having as many offspring as possible. Males supposedly have evolved a preference for mating with women who are physically attractive because these physical characteristics serve as signs in identifying a woman's reproductive value (i.e., she is healthy, youthful, and fertile). Hence, males may be more likely than females to use physical attractiveness as a cue in selecting a possible mate.

The evolutionary perspective does not assume that the choices that females and males make are deliberate, conscious efforts to increase reproductive success. Females may not be thinking, "I need a guy who can make money so my kids will have a better chance of survival," or males, "I need an attractive woman so I can rest assured that she is young and healthy and able to bear plenty of children." Rather, it is assumed that females and males have acquired through the evolutionary process different tendencies and preferences; although these tendencies may be dependent to some extent on context, they will distinguish between females and males across cultures (as demonstrated in Buss, 1989).

There is, of course, variation across cultures in how much females and males differ in their preferences for a potential mate. Also within a culture, women who are economically self-sufficient or who have high-paying professional jobs may be less concerned about the economic resources that a potential mate is able to provide. Nevertheless, results obtained from a variety of countries on different continents (see Figure 2.1 for an example) show that women, compared to men, view the economic resources provided by a prospective mate as important (e.g., has a promising career, has good financial prospects, likely to succeed in profession, likely to earn a lot of money, able to support a mate financially). Men, on the other hand, in a variety of countries consistently value physical attractiveness in a potential mate more than women do (see Figure 2.2).

There may, however, be a gap between stated preferences and actual behavior. Feingold (1990) examined the effects of physical attractiveness on romantic attraction in studies using different research strategies. Although he found that men value and are influenced by physical attractiveness more than women in all types of research, the gender difference in the effects of physical attractiveness was largest in studies using participants' self-reports of preferences (such as in the Buss, 1989, study); it was present but less substantial in studies using behavioral measures (e.g., studies in which participants interact with one another and then rate their interest or liking of partners; studies that look at popularity and physical attractiveness).

In another study, which looked at the effects of education and attractiveness on marriage choices, there was no evidence of gender differences for physically attractive or highly educated marital partners. Stevens, Owens, and Schaefer (1990) rated the educational level and physical attractiveness of 129 couples for whom photographs and descriptive information were presented

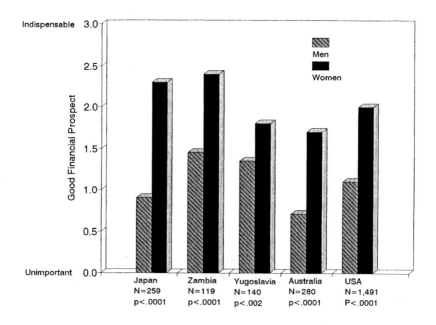

Figure 2.1. Ratings by Women and Men of the Importance of Good
Financial Prospects in a Long-Term Mate or Marriage Partner

SOURCE: From Buss and Schmitt (1993), p. 224. Used by permission of David M. Buss, David
P. Schmitt, and the American Psychological Association.

in newspaper wedding announcements in a U.S. city. The levels of
education and physical attractiveness of one partner were significantly related to the levels of education and physical attractiveness of the other (i.e., there was matching for education and
attractiveness). But physically attractive women were no more
likely than less attractive women to marry a man with a high level
of education. And highly educated men were no more likely than
less educated men to marry a physically attractive woman. Although evolutionary theory predicts that men seek beauty and
women seek resources, there was no indication in this study of
actual marriage choices that either women or men were trading
their preferred characteristic for the preferred characteristic of
their opposite-sex partner.

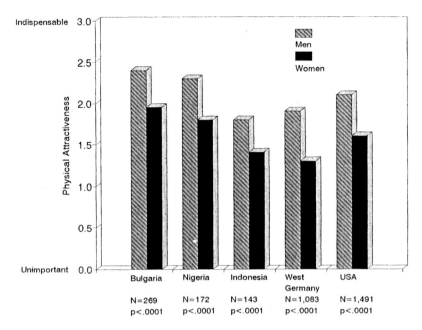

Figure 2.2. Ratings by Women and Men of the Importance of Physical Attractiveness in a Long-Term Mate or Marriage Partner

SOURCE: From Buss and Schmitt (1993), p. 219. Used by permission of David M. Buss, David P. Schmitt, and the American Psychological Association.

Not all dating is "serious." Sometimes we choose a partner or go out just to have fun or, perhaps, in pursuit of a sexual liaison. Do females and males set different standards for a potential partner if they anticipate different levels of a relationship? A recent study by Kenrick, Groth, Trost, and Sadalla (1993) examined men's and women's preferences in a potential partner for a single date, one-night stand, sexual relations, steady dating, and marriage. One set of questions asked about the preferred "status" for a potential partner, based on qualities such as ambition, wealth, college graduate, and earning capacity. For both females and males, there were higher expectations for a partner's status as a relationship increased in involvement. Women also tended to set a higher criterion for status than men across all types of relationships except for a single date. On a measure of attractiveness preferred in a partner (i.e., being physically attractive, sexy, and healthy), men generally held a higher criterion than women at every stage of a relationship except when considering a partner for a one-night stand.

There were a variety of other dimensions along which the men and women were asked to assess a potential partner in Kenrick et al.'s (1993) study, including dominance (e.g., powerful, aggressive), family orientation (e.g., wants children, good housekeeper, and religious), agreeableness (e.g., easygoing, friendly, and understanding), extroversion (e.g., popular, exciting, and sense of humor), intellect (e.g., creative and intelligent), and emotional stability. Assuming that degree of investment increases as partners move from a single date to one-night stand, sexual relations, steady dating, and then marriage, it is interesting that *both* females and males set higher criteria on these characteristics as level of relationship increased. Also, males and females did not generally differ in their criteria for a partner on dominance, family orientation, agreeableness, extroversion, intellect, and emotional stability. However, females, compared to males, set higher criteria on these characteristics, at the level of a one-night stand. If we assume that males, compared to females, associate a one-night stand with a low investment in a relationship whereas females view even a one-night stand as high investment (because of the risk of pregnancy), then the results showing that males set lower standards for such a relationship make sense.

A socialization or social role perspective, however, might argue that these preferences reflect social realities and lessons learned. Females and males recognize that men have greater earning potential than women (in the United States, women make $.70 for every $1 earned by men; U.S. Dept. of Labor Statistics, 1993) and that most women who have children will want the choice of staying out of the workforce for some time or at least of working part-time. But what if couples are nontraditional in their outlook on couplehood, or what if they do not plan to have children, or what if they are gay or lesbian?

Research on gender differences in mate selection has not examined participants' intentions to have or not to have children nor their traditional or nontraditional views of partnership or marriage. A study of personal advertisements by Gonzales and Meyers (1993), however, does provide information about what heterosexual and homosexual men and women seek as well as offer in a possible relationship. Emphasizing the importance of reproduction issues affecting the choice of a partner, heterosexual women were more likely to make appeals for financial security in the ads compared to heterosexual males, homosexual males, and homosexual females. Also, reflecting traditional heterosexual stereotypes, heterosexual men were more likely than homosexual men to offer financial security; heterosexual and homosexual women did not differ in their offer to provide financial security for a partner. It was interesting that no differences were found between the men and women (heterosexual or homosexual) in offers or appeals to physical attractiveness. However, when the advertisements were coded for whether or not physically attractive characteristics were mentioned (e.g., athletic, attractive, cute, slender) heterosexual women used more "attractiveness descriptors" compared to lesbians, whereas gay and heterosexual men did not differ in their use of attractiveness descriptors. Lesbians tend to dismiss traditional assumptions of physical attractiveness as a criterion for selecting a partner. Hence, they may feel less pressured to claim to be attractive (see Gonzales & Meyers, 1993) compared to heterosexual women, who perceive that men judge women in part on the basis of their physical attractiveness.

The results of this study are consistent with the idea that heterosexual men and women (at least in personals ads) may be thinking about a long-term relationship in the search for a partner, where the male may be expected to assume—at least for a time—the role of provider. Hence, the heterosexual women's ads sought a partner who was financially secure, whereas heterosexual men's advertisements seemed to offer financial and occupational stability.

Homosexual men were more likely to make sexually related appeals and offers in their advertisements compared to the other three groups. It is interesting to speculate that the number of sexual references in the ads of homosexual males may be due to the sexual desires of males per se, who in this situation do not have to be cautious in stating their intentions to more sexually conservative females (see Chapter 4).

✿ "Opposites" Attract?

It is sometimes suggested that men and women might be attracted initially to individuals of the opposite sex who demonstrate gender-stereotyped characteristics. For instance, males might be attracted to females who adopt a traditional feminine role (emphasizing nurturance), whereas females might be attracted to males who adopt a traditional masculine role (emphasizing dominance). From a socialization perspective, if males and females have acquired different personal characteristics, then they might find it easier to interact with someone who complements their own personality traits. From an evolutionary perspective, males might prefer nurturance in females because it signals that the woman can take care of children, whereas females might prefer dominance in males because it signals that the man will provide resources and success as a provider and protector for her and their offspring during the time of childrearing.

There is no evidence for sex differences in desire for a marriage or dating partner who is kind and understanding (Buss & Barnes, 1986) or agreeable (Kenrick et al., 1993). It seems that nurturance is something that everyone wants in a partner. There is evidence, however, that dominance may make a bigger difference for females than males in who they choose as a potential partner (at least for a date or in rating sexual desirability). Females are likely to rate a man who exhibits high dominance-type behaviors as more attractive than a man who exhibits low dominance behaviors. Women's dominance-type behaviors have less impact in influencing a male's attraction for a partner (Sadalla, Kenrick, & Vershure, 1987).

We do not want to conclude, however, that (at least in North American culture) dominance in a potential partner is important for females and unimportant for males. When individuals are given information about various combinations of low-high dominance and low-high nurturance, females *and* males rate someone who is relatively high in both dominant (masculine) and nurturant (feminine) characteristics as the most desirable partner and someone who is low in both dominant and nurturant characteristics as the least desirable partner. But consistent with the notion that females weigh dominance more heavily than males when considering a partner for a relationship, females, compared to males, rate a low dominance-high nurturance partner as less desirable (Green & Kenrick, 1994).

✿ Dating

Before Jay leaves the party, he asks Brenda to go out with him the next evening. They talk about going out to eat, but they don't decide where to go afterward. Jay thinks that Brenda might enjoy going to a recently opened country and western bar, where they could listen and dance to live music. He figures that he should check with Brenda when they met to confirm these plans. Jay also wants to make sure that he has enough money to pay for dinner and drinks, so he goes to the bank to cash his last paycheck. The next evening, Jay goes to Brenda's apartment to pick her up for the date. Before they leave Brenda's apartment, they go over their plans for the evening. Then they drive off in Jay's car to a restaurant for dinner.

Traditional gender stereotypes designate the male as assuming the "proactive" role for initiating a relationship and the female as assuming a "reactive" role in accepting or refusing the male's initiatives. These gender roles, particularly for heterosexual men and women, influence sexual behavior in the direction of men overtly initiating physical contact and women adopting a gatekeeper role by deciding whether or not to have sex (Rose & Frieze, 1993).

Gender roles influence courtship between men and women, particularly in the early stages of a relationship when individuals are still getting to know one another. During the early stages of a relationship, couples are more likely to rely on socially defined rules on how to behave. Young adults' behavior is highly scripted along gender lines early in dating (see Rose & Frieze, 1993). For instance, when men and women are asked to describe what happens on a hypothetical "typical" first date, scripts for males are longer than the scripts for females and include more self-directed behavior such as "asking for and planning the date, driving, initiating and paying for date activities, and initiating physical contact" (Rose & Frieze, 1993, p. 501). Scripts for females include more reactive behaviors, such as "specifying that she wait to be asked for a date, be concerned about appearance, keep the conversation going, and reject physical contact" (Rose & Frieze, 1993, p. 501). These descriptions emphasize how males are supposed to "take the initiative" in a first date situation, whereas females are supposed to respond to the male's initiatives.

Although males and females may rely on gender stereotypes to describe what might happen on a hypothetical first date, how do gender roles influence behavior in an actual dating situation? Rose and Frieze (1993) asked female and male undergraduate students to describe, from the beginning to end, what events occurred on an actual first date. A woman's actual first date description more often included waiting to be asked for a date and being concerned about her appearance. On the other hand, a man's actual first date description more often included asking the woman for a date, planning the date, being "courtly" (such as opening doors), paying for expenses on the date, and initiating sexual behavior. Table 2.1 summarizes the descriptions provided by males and females in Rose and Frieze's study (1993) of first dates.

Although there was considerable agreement across individuals about what happens on a first date, there were also departures from what was expected to happen. For instance, 12.7% of individuals reported incidents that deviated from gender stereotypes about what should happen, especially in women's descriptions of violations of gender roles, such as, "He lost points for not opening my car door," or "He never touched me the whole night . . . and I began to wonder about him." Other departures from the "script" for an actual date included: double dating (about 20% of individuals reported that they double dated on their most recent first date); something going wrong (reported by 24.4% of the individuals in the study), such as the male has car trouble after picking up his date and is embarrassed about having to take her

Table 2.1 Actual First-Date Scripts of Heterosexual Women and Men
            Based on Actions Mentioned by 25% of Participants Per
            Script[a]

	Woman's Script	*Man's Script*
	Groomed and dressed	**PICKED UP DATE**[bc]
Man:	**Picked up date**	Met parents/roommates
	Introduced to parents, and so on	**Left**
Man:	Courtly behavior (open doors)	Picked up friends
	Left	**Confirm plans**
	Confirm plans	**TALKED, JOKED, LAUGHED**
	Got to know and evaluate date	**WENT TO MOVIES, SHOW, PARTY**
	TALKED, JOKED, LAUGHED	**ATE**
	Enjoyed date	**Drank alcohol**
	WENT TO MOVIES, SHOW, PARTY	Initiated sexual contact
	ATE	Made out
	Drank alcohol	**TOOK DATE HOME**
	Talked to friends	**Asked for another date**
	Had something go wrong	**KISSED GOODNIGHT**
Man:	**Took date home**	Went home
Man:	**Asked for another date**	
Man:	Told date will call her	
Man:	**Kissed date goodnight**	
	WENT HOME	
Total	14 actions for women 6 actions for men	15 actions for men

a. *N* = 74 women, 61 men.
b. Capital letters indicate the action was mentioned by 50% or more subjects per script.
c. Bold type indicates the action was mentioned for both woman's and man's script.
SOURCE: From Rose and Frieze (1993), p. 505. Used by permission of Suzanna Rose, Irene Hanson Frieze, and Plenum Publishing Company.

back home; or having sex on the first date (reported by 2.2% of the individuals), an action that is not reported when describing a hypothetical first date.

The results of Rose and Frieze's (1993) research indicates that the women saw themselves as highly dependent on the male's behavior in describing what happened on the date. For instance, although everyone was asked to describe "what you did," women were more likely to describe what their male partner had done as well as things they had done themselves, whereas men described only their own actions.

There is considerable controversy about the degree of power men have over women by playing a proactive role in a dating situation (inviting the woman for a date, paying for the date, initiating sex). In particular, when the man pays for everything on the date, the dating situation encourages the man to assume control and the woman to be dependent on him. Furthermore, if males pay all the expenses on a date, they may feel entitled to have sex with their date, and some women may feel pressured to have sex, given this financial arrangement (Muehlenhard, Goggins, Jones, & Satterfield, 1991).

But some women and men are establishing new norms. Sue, a woman in her thirties, divorced and dating again, refuses to let a date pay for everything, partly because she does not want to feel obligated in anyway (sexual or otherwise) to her date. She finds that some men accept or approve of her stance, whereas others are annoyed or even insulted (e.g., "What? You don't think I can afford it?"). Sharing expenses may become the thing to do. (See Box 2.1, A Personal Commentary on Dating in the '90s.)

Traditional gender roles designate men as playing the initiator role and women as playing the reactive role in the first date situation; thus, an interesting question emerges about how much gay men and lesbians will incorporate elements from these roles in their same-sex relations. For instance, gay men and lesbians are less likely than heterosexual men and women to adhere to rigid gender roles about what is considered traditionally to be appropriate behavior for males and females. Also, many gay men place considerable importance on the sexual aspects of a relationship, especially early in a courtship, whereas lesbians tend to emphasize deep emotional involvement even on a first date. Hence, gay men might be more likely to engage in sex on a first date and to be less concerned about intimacy than lesbians.

Klinkenberg and Rose (1994) asked 51 gay men and 44 lesbians to describe their most recent actual first date, that is, "the last time you went out with someone new" (p. 29). Descriptions of actual first dates included some common actions for both the gay men and lesbians, including discuss plans, dress, feeling nervous, get to know date, talk, go to show, eat. However, the actual scripts for the gay men emphasized the sexual aspects of the date (including made out, had sex, and stayed over). About 48% of the men said they had sex on a most recent first date, compared to 12% of the women. See Table 2.2 for a summary of descriptions provided by gay men and lesbians of first dates in Klinkenberg and Rose's (1994) study.

✒ "Being Good at Being a Man (Or Woman)"[1]

The idea that heterosexual men and women are assigned different scripts in dating situations (male script = initiator, female script = reactor) also implies that their performance during dating and courtship may be evaluated by different standards. Women, of course, may run the risk of attacks on their character if their behavior violates gender scripts: Being considered "unladylike" if they don't dress feminine or wear cosmetics; "aggressive" if they take the initiative in setting up a date; and "immoral" if they have sexual intercourse on a first date.

Males may face a challenge to their manhood if they do not live up to cultural standards about how to behave in dating and courtship situations. Men, for instance, express more anxiety about dating than women (Himadi, Arkowitz, Hinton, & Perl, 1980); reflecting concern that it is easier for something to go wrong on a date for the man than the woman and that men are held up to stringent standards of performance.

Although we do not want to overemphasize differences in how males and females are judged during dating and courtship, anthropological research suggests that throughout the world, what it means "to be a man" is judged, in part, by how men behave in social situations. In North American culture, a male who avoids women or who acts shy with women may be ridiculed as a "wimp." In other cultures of the world, sexual shyness or timidity with women may be considered a sign of weakness or "unmanliness." Among the Andalusians of southern Spain, males who measure up as men are referred to as *muy hombre* (very much a man), *muy macho* (very virile), or *mucho hombre* (lots of man). If men don't live

BOX 2.1
A Personal Commentary on Dating in the '90s: Would a Couple Go So Far as to Argue About Who Should Pay for a Date? (This commentary was written by a 22-year-old male who is a recent college graduate)

It's not always the case these days that the man "pops" for dinner and the movie. "Split the bill," "even-steven," "dutch-treat," call it what you will, but the days of one person carrying the financial load of a relationship is mostly a thing of the past. Go on a first date in the 1990s, and there's a good chance that the bill will be split.

It used to be easy. Not long ago the guy was *expected* to pay. Part of chivalry past. Today, it is often considered rude, or even sexist, *not* to allow the woman to carry her equal load when it comes to the final tally. But it's not always clear-cut. What if she's kind of traditional and expects me to pay the bill on the first date? After all, I asked *her* out. But what if she asked me out, would she be the one paying? What if I'm of the mind-set "50-50" all the way, but she didn't bring any money on our first night out? What kind of tension would this create? Just *paying the bill* is not as easy as it may seem.

A lot of younger people approach the topic of paying with financial resourcefulness. Say

you are a college student—money isn't always easy to come by. Both parties involved in a dating scenario know this, although the fact tastefully goes unspoken (or joked about, diffusing the issue). Neither person wants to impose a financial burden, or create economically impossible expectations, so the answer is *split the bill*. He could pay for the first date, but she would pay for the next. Or he'd pay for the cab, and she'd buy desserts. But in the end it all comes out even.

The whole issue is worked out in multiple ways. But let's take the case of Tonya and Adam, who are students at the same university. Adam had long been attracted to Tonya and was pleased when she accepted his invitation to go out. On their first date, he wasn't sure if he'd be paying, but when the dinner bill came, he was the first to move for his wallet, so he paid. "I insist," said Adam. "But let me just pay for my half, I ate less anyway," said Tonya. "No really, I enjoyed your company," he replied. At the movie, Adam

Box 2.1 continued on p. 33

paid again. The date went well. On the next date when the bill came, Adam moved for his wallet, and Tonya dove into her pocketbook. She paid. "You paid last time, so allow me," she said. Seemed reasonable, so an economical decision was reached, and a pattern was set. They'd take turns paying. Not always alternating date-to-date, but a sort of mental total was kept, and each was sure that neither was ever paying too much more than the other.

About 2 months into the relationship, the two hit a financial road-bump in the course of their dating. A special occasion, Valentine's Day. He bought her roses, and she gave him a balloon bouquet. They had agreed on going to a rather expensive Italian restaurant. Appetizers, prima and secondi entrees, dessert, and espresso; the whole nine yards. Dinner took hours, and it was a wonderful night out. But then the bill came. They both moved for their monies. "I'll pay," "No, I'll pay," "Really, let me pay," "I've got it." An economic stand-off. This was such a special evening, both wanted to show their happiness by paying the whole bill. Going dutch wouldn't do in this case. They

looked at each other with a "now what do we do?" look in their eyes. They both set their wallets down on the table and reached for the upside down bill. "You're always paying for everything" Tonya said, although she knew this wasn't really the case. "Oh, come on, just let me pay. You can get the next Valentine's bill," Adam joked.

Tonya really liked Adam, but who'd know if there would be a next Valentine's. They were both thinking this was a petty argument, but it was important to each to pay the bill. Adam took out his credit card, set it on the bill tray, and handed it to the waiter passing by. Tonya sat silent with a disgusted look on her face. Adam signed the bill, and they were off.

Out in the parking lot, Tonya said, "I really wish you'd let me pay"—long pause—"I guess this is our first fight." "I guess you're right," replied Adam. He opened her car door, and they drove off.

In the end, Tonya did pay for the next year's Valentine's night out on a chartered sailboat. The two laughed about last Valentine's Day and their first argument.

Table 2.2 Scripts for Actual First Dates of Lesbian Women and Gay Men Based on Actions Mentioned by 25% of Participants Per Script

Lesbians (N = 25)	Gay Men (N = 23)
DISCUSSED PLANS[ab]	DISCUSSED PLANS
Was nervous	Was nervous
GROOMED/DRESSED	GROOMED/DRESSED
Prepared (cleaned apartment, bought flowers, etc.)	Went to date's house/Picked up date
Went to date's house/Picked up date	Met at pre-arranged location
P[c]: Went to date's house/Picked up date	Left one location for another
Left	GOT TO KNOW/EVALUATED DATE
GOT TO KNOW/ EVALUATED DATE	TALKED/LAUGHED/ JOKED
TALKED/LAUGHED/ JOKED	Talked to friends while on date
WENT TO A MOVIE, SHOW, ETC.	WENT TO A MOVIE, SHOW, ETC.
ATE/DRANK NON-ALCOHOL	ATE/DRANK NON-ALCOHOL
Positive affect	DRANK ALCOHOL/USED DRUGS
Drank alcohol/used drugs	INITIATED PHYSICAL CONTACT
INITIATED PHYSICAL CONTACT	Made out
Kissed/hugged goodnight	Had sex
Took date home	Stayed over
Went home	Made plans for another date
P: Went home	Went home
Evaluate feelings post-date	

a. Capital letters indicate script actions were cited by 50% or more participants.
b. Bold type indicates the action is common to both gay men and lesbians.
c. Indicates partner-initiated action.
SOURCE: From Klinkenberg and Rose (1994), p. 30. Used by permission of Dean Klinkenberg, Suzanna Rose, and Haworth Press.

up to standards of performance (including being successful in wooing women), then they are *flojo* (a weak and pathetic impostor; see Gilmore, 1990, p. 32). There is a similar expectation in cultures throughout the world that men must demonstrate their worth by taking charge and perhaps playing an assertive (even aggressive) role in dating and courtship (Gilmore, 1990). A man who objects to his date's preference for sharing the bill probably has accepted the belief that his manhood is reflected in his ability to pay.

There is something paradoxical and a possible source of conflict in male-female relationships between what characteristics are sought in a partner and what behaviors are allowed—at least early in a dating relationship. Whereas men and women aspire for a partner who has good social-emotional skills (e.g., kindness, gentleness, and friendliness) and who is assertive and confident interpersonally, many men and women fear acting in ways that defy gender stereotypes. It is often taken for granted that men should take charge of the date and that women should respond to a situation that is orchestrated by the man. Unfortunately, this arrangement favors men who are comfortable being assertive interpersonally—regardless of their social-emotional skills, and it may penalize women who are skilled in being interpersonally assertive (see Kenrick, 1994, pp. 108-110).

We have described the impact of gender on the choice of a romantic partner and on expectations and behavior in a dating situation. Next, we consider how gender influences couples' decisions about a practical matter in dating—the use of condoms.

⊯ "Safer Sex": Condom Use Among Dating Couples

Jay and Brenda have gone out together several times, and after a month of dating, they decide to have sex. Jay and Brenda use condoms, as a protection against pregnancy and the possibility of sexually transmitted diseases (STDs). (Jay has bought a box of condoms at a local drugstore a short time before he and Brenda first have intercourse, just so they would have it available in case [or when] they were sexually intimate.) Jay and Brenda continue to use condoms for several months. Eventually, they begin to think of themselves as a "steady couple." At that point, Brenda begins to take birth control pills that she obtains from her physician. Jay and Brenda don't really consider themselves to be at risk for STDs (including HIV), and since Brenda is now on the pill, they don't think they need to worry anymore about an unwanted pregnancy.

Decisions about the use of condoms represent a major issue (and a possible source of strain) for couples. Although many heterosexual couples use condoms out of concern about an unwanted pregnancy, they may also use condoms to reduce the risk of HIV infection and other STDs such as genital herpes, genital warts, or chlamydia (Nevid, 1995). However, many couples put themselves at risk for STDs and an unwanted pregnancy because of unsafe sexual practices. For instance, Fisher and Fisher (1990) conducted a survey of sexual behavior on a college campus. They found that 72% of college students had been sexually active during the previous 12 months. Among those who had been sexually active, 75% did not use condoms consistently when they had sexual intercourse, and 44% of the sexually active individuals had two or more partners.

Males' and females' attitudes about condoms may help us understand why couples feel more or less comfortable using them when they have sexual intercourse. Many men and women associate the use of condoms with being a caring and responsible sexual partner; but these positive views ("I associate condoms with a caring partner" and "I associate condoms with responsibility") are more likely to be held by females than males. On the other hand, men are more likely than women to endorse negative attitudes about condoms. Men are more likely to agree with statements such as, "talking about condoms is a threat to the relationship itself" or "condom use reduces pleasure" and "condoms are uncomfortable" (cf. Cline & McKenzie, 1994).

Males are traditionally expected to exercise more initiative, especially early in a heterosexual relationship (including initiating sexual behaviors, although women can slow down or reject the male's initiatives or use indirect cues to signal their interest in having sex). If males assume a more powerful role than women early in a relationship, a man's attitudes about condoms may have more impact than a woman's attitudes on whether they discuss or use condoms, especially with a new or casual partner (see Galligan & Terry, 1993). This point is illustrated in the following comment provided by a 25-year-old woman about her efforts to have male partners use condoms:

> I have had problems asking men to use condoms even though I know using condoms is the right thing to do to reduce the risk of AIDS or other STDs. Guys will complain that a condom doesn't feel comfortable or they say "we're safe." When I thought I might have sex with someone I really liked, I went out and bought a box of condoms. He

> looked at me suspiciously when I showed him the condoms . . . as if I would have sex with anyone.

A study by Galligan and Terry (1993) looked at the connection between attitudes about condoms and discussion of or use of condoms. They found that males' attitudes about condoms were more likely than females' attitudes to predict discussion or condom usage, especially with new or casual sexual partners. Males' belief that friends and/or partners think they should use a condom when having sex (i.e., social norms) also influenced behavior more than females' beliefs did. These findings suggest that the male role of initiator in dating and sexual relations also gives males more influence on whether or not condoms are discussed or used. In steady relationships, the difference between male and female influence was not as great. As we will see in Chapter 4, male initiation of sexual relationships is also less pronounced in committed relationships.

A final comment is worth making about the link between how close partners feel about one another and how likely they are to use condoms. There is diversity in condom use among dating couples, but research indicates that individuals are two to three times more likely to report always using condoms with a new or casual dating partner than with someone with whom they have a steady relationship (Catania, Coates, & Kegeles, 1994). A commitment to using condoms with a new or casual dating partner may be motivated by a desire to provide protection against pregnancy or the transmission of STDs (including HIV and genital herpes). But as individuals begin trusting and caring for one another, getting HIV and other STDs stops being a concern. The following rule of thumb may emerge among couples who know and like one another: "When you get to know the person . . . as soon as you trust the person . . . you don't really have to use a condom" (Williams et al., 1993, p. 926). When opposite-sex couples feel positively about their relationships, they are likely to be concerned only about an unwanted pregnancy. Then the couples are likely to rely on a female mode of contraception, such as birth control pills. Gay men are also likely to stop using condoms as they develop positive feelings toward their partner, despite the heightened risk of AIDS in the gay population (Gold, Skinner, & Ross, 1994; Kelly et al., 1991). Unfortunately, among heterosexual or homosexual women and men, being trustworthy and lovable may be unrelated to the presence of sexually transmittable viruses.

⁊ Perceived Benefits and Costs of Romantic Relationships

Jay and Brenda have been dating for 6 months. They have enjoyed being together. They have even talked about sharing an apartment during the next school year. There have been some minor problems, however. Brenda likes to spend evenings reading, and she would like Jay to be with her. Jay, on the other hand, enjoys watching sports events on television. He would like to spend a couple of evenings each week watching TV sports programs with his male friends. On the other hand, Jay feels left out when Brenda says she is not available to be with him (e.g., Brenda spent the last weekend helping a female friend look for a new car, while Jay "hung out" alone in his apartment).

As couples develop romantic relationships, they are likely to experience many positive outcomes (including the pleasures associated with feeling close and connected with their partner). On the other hand, as partners become "connected," they may also feel that they have sacrificed their individual autonomy or independence. A question then emerges about the similarities and differences in men and women about what they perceive as the benefits and costs of seriously dating one person or sustaining a romantic relationship. Both men and women may feel that a close romantic relationship is beneficial because they can obtain companionship, sexual gratification, and the feeling of being loved. On the other hand, if men, compared to women, have a greater interest in sexual activity as a goal, they might rate sexual gratification more frequently as a benefit of a romantic relationship than females. Also, if women place a greater value on emotional involvement and commitment in a romantic relationship as important to their self-worth, females might rate positive self-esteem and loss of self-esteem more frequently as a benefit and cost, respectively, of romantic relationships than males.

A study by Sedikides, Oliver, and Campbell (1994) provides interesting data about the perceived benefits and costs of romantic relationships for young men and women. Heterosexual individuals were asked to provide information about the "most important benefits" they enjoyed and the "most serious costs" they suffered as a result of their romantic relationships. Companionship or affiliation was the most frequently mentioned benefit of a romantic relationship (mentioned by 60% of participants in the study). Sexual satisfaction (46%), feeling loved or loving another (43%), intimacy (42%), and expertise in relationships (40%) were also frequently mentioned as benefits. In contrast, the lack of freedom to socialize (69%) and lack of freedom to date (68%) were the most frequently mentioned costs of a romantic relationship for both men and women.

Although there were many similarities between men and women in perceived rewards and costs, there were some differences that are worth noting. Males (65%) were more likely than females (26%) to mention sexual gratification as an important benefit they enjoyed in romantic relationships. Women (49%) were more likely than men (14%) to mention positive self-esteem (such as "higher self-respect and self-confidence") as an important benefit. Although both males and females mentioned the lack of freedom to socialize and lack of freedom to date as the most serious costs they suffered in romantic relationships, males, compared to females, mentioned these costs more frequently. Males (18%) were more likely to mention monetary losses as a cost than females (6%) did, whereas females were more likely than males to mention loss of identity (29% versus 14%), feeling worse about the self (29% versus 14%) and increased dependence on the partner (23% versus 3%) as costs of romantic relationships.

In general, men were more likely than women to perceive that they were making a social sacrifice to have a romantic relationship. They were also somewhat more likely to perceive that they were making a financial sacrifice, perhaps reflecting the traditional view that men assume greater responsibility for expenses associated with dating. (Recall, however, that only 18% of the males and 6% of the females mentioned monetary losses as an important cost.)

To the extent that women, compared to men, identify their self-worth with romantic relationships, it also makes sense that women mentioned more positive self-esteem (as a perceived benefit) and feeling worse about the self (as a perceived cost). It seems that what happens in a romantic relationship has greater significance for how women feel about themselves. Women were also more likely than men to mention loss of identity and increased dependence on the partner as perceived costs. Perhaps women more than men perceive that they have to give up something about themselves to be in a romantic relationship. The loss of identity experienced by some women in a romantic relationship may be due to the perception that they have a less powerful position than men in romantic relationships or that women are expected to be more responsive and concerned about the emotional needs of their male partner than vice versa (see Josephs, Markus, & Tafarodi, 1992, for additional discussion of these issues).

ᴥ Conclusions

It may be that women and men have been influenced historically by different reproductive strategies and cultural traditions about *who* to seek as a partner in a dating or romantic relationship. The importance of these biological and cultural factors in the selection of dating and romantic partners may be diminishing in recent years, especially as the average couple might expect both partners to work outside the home and to contribute to the family income. Nevertheless, especially in the early stages of a dating relationship and courtship, women's and men's behavior seems to be influenced by gender scripts. The challenge for relationship partners is to create their own identity as partners where they don't need to act in terms of culture-linked gender stereotypes but rather in response to one another's personal needs and wishes.

ᴥ Note

1. This subheading title is adopted from Michael Herzfeld's (1985) book, *The Poetics of Manhood: Contest and Identity in a Cretan Mountain Village* (p. 16).

3

Sexual Relations

Gender has a major impact on sexual behavior in relationships. Males and females have obvious physiological differences that affect sexuality (the major organ for sexual arousal is the penis for men, and the clitoris and lower third of the vagina for women; women can experience repeated or multiple orgasms more easily then males can; women can become pregnant, men cannot). However, the behavior and meaning of sexuality for men and women in relationships is also influenced by their learning experiences in a particular culture and, perhaps, by strategies of mating acquired through the evolution of the human species. Men and women report pursuing somewhat different goals in their sexual activities. Young men more than women seem to have physical gratification as a goal. Women also focus on the physical pleasure associated with sexual behaviors, but women more than men prefer sex in an emotionally close or committed relationship.

In this chapter, we will examine how these different orientations toward sexuality affect women's and men's relationships.

The topics that we cover in this chapter include: male and female attitudes about what is acceptable sexual behavior in a relationship; why men more than women seek sex in casual relationships; how social norms affect what men and women do in their sexual behavior; and how gender-linked attitudes about sexuality may be associated with sexual aggression.

❧ Male and Female Attitudes About Acceptable Sexual Behaviors

> I don't like it when someone I am starting to date goes right away for my breasts and genitals. I want to move more gradually into sex as I get to know my partner. (Woman, 22 years old)

> I would prefer to have sex in a loving relationship. But I think that sex is a good thing in itself. I don't need to feel emotionally close to someone to be comfortable and enjoy sex. (Man, 28 years old)

The context of a relationship (e.g., casual versus serious) is extremely important for most people in evaluating sexual activity (Bettor, Hendrick, & Hendrick, 1995). But research indicates that men and women may hold different attitudes about what is acceptable sexual behavior—especially in the beginning or early stages of a relationship. For instance, Knox and Wilson (1981) asked college students in North Carolina how many dates they felt they should have with someone before it was appropriate to engage in kissing, petting, and intercourse. There was little difference between the men and women concerning when it was appropriate for kissing to occur. About 14% of the men and women felt that no dates were necessary for kissing to occur, whereas 55% of the women and 69% of the men felt that kissing on the first date was appropriate. By the time of the fourth date, all but 3% of the women felt that kissing was appropriate.

There was more concern that petting ("hands anywhere") be delayed, especially by the women. More than 75% of the women felt that petting should be delayed until after the fourth date whereas only 35% of the men felt that way. Instead, almost one third of the men felt that petting was appropriate before or on the first date.

There was also evidence that men wanted to have intercourse sooner in the dating relationship than women. Whereas almost half of the men rated intercourse as appropriate by the fifth date, only about one fourth of the women agreed with them.

Knox and Wilson (1981) also asked the college students in their study about the degree of emotional involvement that should exist when kissing, petting, and intercourse occur. The levels of emotional involvement or intimacy were feeling no particular affection, feeling affection but not love, being in love, engaged, or married. For both men and women, the more emotionally involved the individuals were in a relationship, the more likely that sexual intimacy was perceived as appropriate. This link was stronger for women than men. For instance, 10% of the men indicated that intercourse without any affection was all right, but only about 1% of the women felt this way. Thus, the women were more concerned than the men about the emotional relationship in which sexual intimacy occurred.

A study by Sprecher (1989) also indicated that men more than women view sex as acceptable early in a relationship, but that men and women tend to hold similar attitudes about acceptable sexual behavior later in a relationship. College students at a midwestern American university were asked about the acceptability for themselves of heavy petting (touching the genitals), intercourse, and oral-genital sex in a relationship. Males, more than females, reported that these sexual activities were acceptable on a first date or when casually dating. However, there were no gender differences in what was considered acceptable sexual behavior in a serious dating relationship or if the couple were engaged. These results support the view that men are more likely to consider sex as OK (whether sex occurs in a casual or loving relationship), but women are more likely to view sex as acceptable in the context of a committed or emotionally based relationship such as serious dating or being engaged.

A series of studies conducted by Buss and Schmitt (1993) support the conclusion that young men are more accepting than young women of sex in casual relationships. A group of female and male college students at a midwestern university was asked:

> If the conditions were right, would you consider having sexual intercourse with someone you viewed as desirable . . . if you had known that person for 5 years . . . if you had known that person for 2 years . . . if you had known that person for 1 year . . . if you had known that person for 6 months . . . if you had known that person for 3 months . . . 1 month . . . 1 week . . . 1 day . . . 1 evening . . . 1 hour?

Ratings were made on a scale with responses running from –3 = *definitely not* to 3 = *definitely yes.* See the results in Figure 3.1.

The shorter the time interval that the potential partner is known, the more likely that men, compared to women, were willing to engage in intercourse. For instance, if the partner was known for just 1 week, the males felt slightly positive about having sex, whereas women felt highly negative about having sex. If the potential partner was known just for an hour, men were only slightly opposed to having sex, whereas women were definitely opposed to having sex.

A second group of college students studied by Buss and Schmitt (1993) was asked about their interest in finding a partner for a one-night stand or a brief affair (i.e., a "short-term" partner) as well as finding someone to marry (i.e., a "long-term" partner). Males and females did not differ in how interested they were in finding a long-term partner, but males more than females reported that they were interested in finding a partner for a short-term sexual relationship.

If sex itself as a goal is more important for males than females, males might also desire to have more sexual partners than females want to have. A third group of undergraduate students studied by Buss and Schmitt (1993) was asked how many sexual partners they would ideally like to have during various time intervals, for example, during the next month, 6 months, 1 year, 2 years, 3 years, 4 years, 5 years, 10 years, 30 years, and over a lifetime. Consistent with the idea that sex as an activity is more important for men than women, men wanted more sexual partners than the women wanted over the various time intervals. See the results in

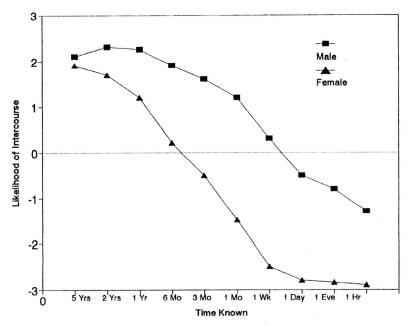

Figure 3.1. Ratings by Women and Men of Likelihood of Consenting to Sexual Intercourse

SOURCE: From Buss and Schmitt (1993), p. 221. Used by permission of David M. Buss, David P. Schmitt, and the American Psychological Association.

Figure 3.2. For instance, over the next 2 years, males wanted to have 8 sexual partners, whereas females wanted about one sexual partner. Over the period of a lifetime, men indicated a desire for more than 18 sexual partners, whereas women indicated a desire for about 4 or 5 partners.

If men more than women say they are interested in having sex with someone in a casual relationship, would they actually jump at such an invitation if approached by an attractive stranger in a public situation? This idea was tested in research conducted by Clark (1990). An attractive male or female confederate (who was a research assistant of the experimenter) approached strangers of the other sex on a college campus. The confederate said, "I have been noticing you around campus. I find you to be very attractive." Then the confederate asked one of three questions: Would

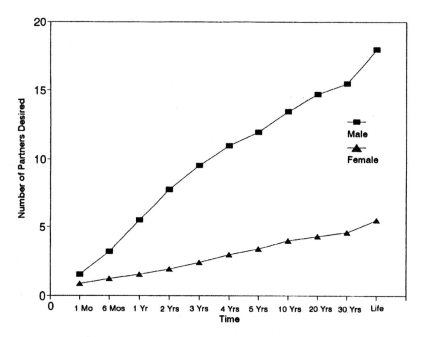

Figure 3.2. Ratings by Women and Men of the Number of Sexual Partners Desired

SOURCE: From Buss and Schmitt (1993), p. 221. Used by permission of David M. Buss, David P. Schmitt, and the American Psychological Association.

you go out with me tonight? Would you come over to my apartment tonight? or Would you go to bed with me tonight? The invitations were made during weekdays to decrease the likelihood that the research participants might have had other social obligations or dates planned. When the women were approached for a date, 44% agreed to go on this date, whereas 14% accepted the invitation to go to the man's apartment, and no one consented to the request to have sex. Among the men, 69% agreed to go on a date, 50% agreed to go back to the woman's apartment, and 69% consented to go have sex with her. In similar research conducted by Clark and Hatfield (1989), female confederates reported that many males seemed to be comfortable with the invitation to have sex. Men's typical responses included, "Why do we have to wait until tonight?" or "I cannot tonight, but tomorrow would be fine."

Clark and Hatfield (1989) also found that men were more likely than women to give apologies when they said no, for example, "I'm married" or "I'm going with someone." When women responded to the invitation by the male to go to bed, they were more likely to say, "You've got to be kidding" or "What is wrong with you? Leave me alone." Of course, it is not true that every man will consent to an invitation to have casual sex, or that every woman will turn down such an invitation. Nevertheless, the research by Clark (1990) and Clark and Hatfield (1989) provides behavioral evidence that males are more willing than females to have sex in a casual relationship.

It is important to note that *all* the studies reported in this section have been done using college students as their subjects. As we will see later in this chapter, older females and males may have different views about their motives for sex. Although it is clear that males are more accepting of and interested in sex in casual relationships, even with strangers, than females are, we should be cautious about generalizing these findings to all adults.

ǖ Why Men and Women Hold Different Attitudes About Sex in Casual Relationships

Why do young men more than young women value sex as an activity in itself and without restrictions about the type of relationship that might exist with the partner? We will consider some possible explanations.

Reproductive Strategies. This view holds that men and women are genetically programmed to be either interested in or restrained about having sex. Men and women are supposed to obtain a genetic advantage by producing as many offspring as possible. However, they may have a different reproductive strategy because of the different investment they must make to have children. A man can sire numerous children, whereas a woman can give birth to and raise only a limited number of children. Women make a greater investment than men in having and raising children (e.g., fertilization, implantation, and gestation of the fertilized ovum occur internally within women and breast-feeding may extend for several years after the baby's birth in many societies). Although many men may invest heavily in having and raising children (e.g., earning an income to support the child), the minimum investment necessary by a man is to contribute the sperm. Hence, from an evolutionary view, women compared to men should disapprove of casual sex and have fewer sexual partners. Women should be selective about whom they have sex with in order to ensure the best possible male genes for offspring and have a male partner who would commit himself to assist in raising children with the mother. Men, on the other hand, should be more approving of casual sex and have more sexual partners because they can maximize their reproductive advantage by having sex with and impregnating as many women as possible.

Early Adolescent Sexual Experiences. Physical pleasure in sex may be the focus for men more often than for women because of early adolescent sexual experiences. Males are more likely than females to masturbate at the beginning of puberty. Surveys suggest that, by age 13, 63% of males have masturbated, but only 32% to 33% of females have done so (Hunt, 1974, and Bell, Weinberg, & Hammersmith, 1981, as reported by DeLamater, 1987). Males' masturbatory experiences highlight the physical and pleasurable aspects of sexuality: the boy takes the flaccid penis in his hand, strokes it, has an erection, and ejaculates, which results in orgasm. The boy's early sexual experiences with masturbation may lead him to believe that ejaculation and orgasm should be the "prototype" for his future sexual experiences (see Gagnon & Simon, 1973, pp. 62-64). On the other hand, females are much less likely to masturbate in early adolescence and even these early masturbatory experiences are different from what happens in heterosexual contacts (girls usually masturbate by stroking the clitoris and labia with their fingers and tightening their hips and thighs around a pillow or a similar object). Girls do not usually insert their finger or an object inside the vagina. Rook and Hammen (1977) have argued that masturbation provides direct experiences with sexual arousal and gratification. But this direct experience, while being more frequent for males than females, may also be more similar to the experiences males have in heterosexual encounters. Girls' masturbatory experiences, stimulating the clitoris and labia, may not mimic their experiences with heterosexual intercourse.

The onset of puberty is experienced differently by females and males. The first signs of sexual maturation for males, in addition to secondary sex characteristics (e.g., body hair, voice changes), are nocturnal emissions (i.e., wet dreams), which are likely to be experienced as physically pleasurable, if sometimes confusing and embarrassing. They are directly related to sexual arousal and release and often lead to masturbation. The first sign of sexual maturation for females, in addition to secondary sex characteristics, is menarche, that is, the beginning of menstruation. Menstruation is unrelated to sexual arousal or pleasure and is viewed as a sign of reproductive maturation ("now you can get pregnant") rather than as having to do with sexual behavior, except perhaps as a warning to avoid it.

Female adolescents are less likely to masturbate and thus have less direct experience with sexual arousal and orgasm. They are likely to view their sexual maturation in terms of the possibility of becoming pregnant. Both of these circumstances may contribute to women being less likely than men to view the physical pleasure of sex as a goal in itself and less likely to seek sex in casual relationships.

Gender Roles. There may be social pressures that encourage males more than females to focus on sexual activity itself and to isolate sex from emotional intimacy with their relationship partner. A dominant theme in North American culture holds that males should be successful in work and that success is represented by achieving specific goals. Males may become preoccupied with sexual activity (including the goal of achieving orgasm in sexual encounters and having many sexual partners) as they seek to fulfill the male role. Thus, more traditional attitudes about masculinity among males should be associated with greater willingness to participate in casual sex. Consistent with this view, a nationwide survey of adolescent males in the United States found that males who endorsed a traditional male role (e.g., "It is essential for a guy to get respect from others," "A young man should be physically tough, even if he's not big," and "I don't think a husband should have to do housework"), compared to males who rejected a traditional male role, had more sexual partners in the last year and reported being less emotionally involved with the most recent partner with whom they had intercourse (Pleck, Sonenstein, & Ku, 1993b).

A double standard may also affect women. It is common for students to report that a person who has many sexual partners is a "stud" if he is male, but a "slut" if she is female. Sprecher, McKinney, and Orbuch (1987) provide empirical evidence for a double standard for females and males having sex in casual relationships. When college students rated a woman or man having first coitus in a casual or a close relationship, the woman was more negatively rated, especially on general personality characteristics, than the man when the relationship was casual (Sprecher et al., 1987).

Concerns for Personal Safety. It is possible that many men *and* women might be interested in having sex in a casual relationship, but women more than men are concerned about their personal safety. Women may be more fearful of being sexually assaulted or injured by a stranger or a casual acquaintance, which makes them less likely to accept a sexual invitation from a stranger or to have many sexual partners. Men, on the other hand, may be less concerned about being physically harmed, which makes them more adventurous sexually in casual relationships.

❧ Reasons Given by Females and Males for Having Sex

I was a virgin when I started dating my boyfriend, Bill, in high school. We had been going out for 5 months. We had enjoyed heavy petting, but I did not want to be pushed into making love until I was ready. I wanted to feel real close or even that I loved him before we had intercourse. When we made love for the first time, I knew that I cared for him a lot and that he felt the same way about me. (25-year-old woman, describing her first intercourse when she was 17 years old)

The first time I had intercourse, I was a junior in high school, and I was dating this woman who was a senior. She had sex already with two different guys, and so she was more experienced than I was. We went out a few times, but it didn't take long before we had intercourse together. I guess I didn't feel that I loved her or that we were in a committed relationship. I was just excited at the opportunity to have sex. (23-year-old man, describing his first sexual experience when he was 16 years old)

Sex with my boyfriend is extremely satisfying. We do a lot of sweating, panting, and squirming. I wish though that we would talk more about sex after it was over. I would like him to say more often to me that it felt real special or that he loved making love with me. (Woman, 26 years old)

My girlfriend, Peggy, and I are really close to one another. But I feel that we have to do a better job trying to accommodate one another when we are having sex. I get aroused very quickly. When I have an erection, I am ready for intercourse or oral sex. Peggy, on the other had, wants me to slow down and spend more time caressing and hugging her. Sometimes she even wants us to put on romantic music and light candles to set the mood for having sex. I guess I am more eager to get down to business, and she's more interested in the setting. (Man, 23 years old)

In this section, we will report on the different reasons and motives that men and women give for having sex. First, as evidence about gender differences in motivations for having sex, let us consider the type of relationship that exists when females and males who are virgins have their first coital experience. Table 3.1 present some typical findings about female-male differences in the quality of the relationship when intercourse occurred for the first time.

Both women and men are likely to have first intercourse in an emotionally close relationship (i.e., with a steady partner, a fiancé, or someone they love). However, this first intercourse experience in an emotionally close relationship is more likely to occur for women than for men. For instance, women more than men are likely to report that the first coital experience occurred with a steady partner. On the other hand, men more than women are likely to report that the first coital experience occurred with an

Table 3.1 Type of Relationship With First Sexual Partner

	Source			
	Darling, Davidson, & Passarelo, 1992		Faulkenberry, Vincent, James, & Johnson, 1987	
Partner Relationship	Female	Male	Female	Male
Steady partner	66.1%	43.5%	68%	42%
Acquaintance	12.8%	32.6%	18%	45%
Just met person or unknown partner	3.7%	13%	1%	7%
Engaged partner or lover	15.6%	10.9%	12%	3%
Relative	1.8%		1%	3%

NOTE: The data are derived from questionnaires administered to unmarried American undergraduate students. Data are used by permission of Carol A. Darling, J. Kenneth Davidson, Sr., Lauren C. Passarello, and Plenum Press and from J. Ron Faulkenberry and Libra Publisher, Inc.

acquaintance or someone they just met or did not know. These results are consistent with the view that males are more likely to desire sex as an end in itself (a physical gratification motive), whereas females are more likely to desire sex as an expression of love and intimacy in a relationship (a relationship-expression motive). (Michael, Gagnon, Laumann, & Kolata, 1994, pp. 92-93, report similar results in a recent nationwide survey in the United States.)

There are different reasons for having sex. Individuals can have sex to feel close to their partner, for pure pleasure, for tension release, and so forth. Women and men tend to give different reasons for having sex.

A study conducted by Leigh (1989) among heterosexual and homosexual individuals illustrates how gender affects someone's reasons for having sex, regardless of her or his sexual orientation. Individuals living in the San Francisco area were asked about their reasons for having sex. Males, compared to females, placed more importance on having sex for pure pleasure, to please one's partner, for conquest, and to relieve sexual tension. Females, compared to males, placed more importance on the desire to express emotional closeness. These gender differences occurred for the heterosexual and homosexual participants in the study, supporting the view that there may be differences between men and women in motivations for having sex regardless of their sexual orientation. Men—gay or straight—tended to focus on physical gratification, and women—lesbian or straight—tended to focus on emotional intimacy in making decisions to have sex with someone. It was interesting in Leigh's study that men more than women rated pleasing the partner as important. This gender difference was stronger for the heterosexual than the gay/lesbian participants in the research. It appears that concern for the partner's pleasure is greater for men in heterosexual than in gay relationships, reflecting perhaps the perception that male sexual performance extends to ensuring the woman's sexual pleasure.

A study by Hatfield, Sprecher, Pillermer, Greenberger, and Wexler (1988) shows that male-female differences in motivations for sex extend to what individuals want their partner to do for them. Individuals in dating and married relationships were asked to rate what they wanted from their partner during sex. In both dating and married samples, females more than males indicated that they wanted their partner to talk more lovingly during sex. In both dating and married samples, on the other hand, males more than females indicated that they wanted activities that emphasized physical arousal and excitement, including to "be more rough, more experimental, more willing to engage in fast, impulsive sex, initiate sex more, and play the dominant role in sex more" (Hatfield et al., 1988, p. 45). In the dating couples, the biggest gender difference was for the males more than the females to desire more initiative from the partner when having sex. In the married couples, the biggest gender difference was for the males more than the females to desire fast and impulsive sex. Men wanted sexual activities to increase their physical gratification, whereas women wanted sexual activities to increase intimacy and love in the relationship.

Men's motives for engaging in sexual intercourse emphasize physical reasons (e.g., pleasure, relieve sexual tension), whereas women's motives emphasize emotional reasons (e.g., commitment and love). There is evidence, however, that gender differences in motivations for engaging in sexual intercourse depend on age. Sprague and Quadagno (1989) studied the motivations for initiating sex among a group of adults aged 22 to 57 years. In the 22- to 35-year-old age group, men were more likely than women to say that they engaged in sex because they wanted the physical release (physical motive), whereas the women were more likely to say that they engaged in sex to show love for their partner (love motive). On the other hand, in the 36- to 57-year-old age group, men were less likely than women to say that they engaged in sex for the physical release, whereas males were more likely than females to say that they engaged in sex to show love. These results suggest that age may have an impact on the character of women's and men's sexual motivation. Men and women may learn "scripts" in adolescence and early adulthood that men are supposed to focus on the physical aspects of sex and women on emotional concerns. As men and women grow older, they may be less concerned with fulfilling cultural stereotypes about what is acceptable and desirable sexual behavior in their relationships. Hence, women can give more attention to the physical aspects of sex and men can give more attention to the emotional aspects of sex as they get older.

The research we have summarized suggests that men believe sex should not be restricted by type of relationship or emotional involvement, whereas women believe that sex should occur in an emotionally close relationship. However, these results do not mean that sex in close relationships is important for women and unimportant for men. Research by Cate, Long, Angera, and Draper (1993) found that weighing considerations about the quality of the relationship in the decision to have sex with a partner for the first time (e.g., "How much do you love your partner?" "How much have you discussed the meaning of sexual intercourse with your partner?") was associated with how much the relationship improved after having intercourse for both women *and* men. Men and women may differ on the average in how much they value physical pleasure and emotional closeness as goals in a sexual encounter. But, for both males and females, whether the relationship improves or worsens after having intercourse is affected by prior feelings about their partner and the relationship.

⅋ Sexual Role-Playing: Who Initiates, Who Sets Limits?

Traditional gender norms assume that men and women play different roles in their sexual interactions. Men are expected to initiate sex within a relationship (the initiator role), whereas women are expected to act as limit setters by either refusing "his" requests for sex or by determining when they will have sex (the restrictor role). Most men and women tend to share similar attitudes about acceptable sexual behavior in a close relationship (e.g., when couples are steady dating partners, in love, or living together). However, traditional gender stereotypes about who should initiate sex and who should set limits may still operate.

A pioneering study by Peplau, Rubin, and Hill (1977) illustrates how traditional gender roles influence heterosexual couples' decisions to have intercourse for the first time. Peplau and her associates predicted that if the man is expected to initiate sex and the woman is expected to set limits, the woman's attitudes and preferences would influence whether a couple has sexual intercourse, and—for couples who have intercourse—when or how soon in the relationship intercourse should occur for the first time.

Peplau et al. (1977) studied 231 college-age dating couples in the Boston metropolitan area. At the beginning of the research, the typical couple had been dating about 8 months. There were 42 couples (or 18% of the sample) who had abstained from intercourse. These "abstaining couples" were much more conservative than sexually active couples in their attitudes about sexual conduct. However, the males in these abstaining couples usually wanted to have sex, but the women were less interested. For instance, the men (64%) were more likely than the women (11%) to indicate that their partner's wish not to have sex was a major reason for the couple's abstinence. The women (31%) in the abstaining couples were also more likely than the men (11%) to say that having intercourse was a violation of their ethical standards.

About 82% of the couples in Peplau et al.'s (1977) study had intercourse in their present relationship. Among these couples it was found that the woman's attitudes and preferences influenced when coitus first occurred. Generally couples who had intercourse within a month of the first date were more accepting of having sex in a casual relationship compared to couples who had intercourse later in their relationship. However, for women only, conservative social attitudes predicted the timing of intercourse. For instance, women who had intercourse early in the relationship were less likely to rate themselves as being religious or to want to be a full-time housewife. They were also likely to rate themselves higher on reactivity, intelligence, self-confidence, and desirability as a date.

When couples first had intercourse together was influenced by both partners' previous sexual experience. However, the woman's sexual experience had more impact than the man's sexual experience in determining the timing of first intercourse in the relationship. When the woman was sexually experienced, the couple had intercourse within a shorter time of starting the relationship than when the woman was a virgin.

Peplau et al.'s (1977) results indicate, overall, that men's interest in and willingness to suggest having sex at some point in the couples' relationship was a "relatively constant factor." The woman played the role of limit-setter in determining if and when the couple had sexual intercourse.

What happens if a couple is already having intercourse in their current relationship? Do men and women still rely on traditional gender norms to decide who initiates or who restricts sexual activities? Are men, compared to women, more likely to initiate sexual activity and to accept every available chance to have sex? Are women, compared to men, more likely to try to play the role of gatekeeper in controlling men's sexual access to them? Also, do women have to use indirect methods of indicating an interest in sexual activity because men—and not women—are expected to initiate sexual activity? Recent research indicates that sexual interactions among men and women still appear to be influenced in part by traditional sexual scripts about how men and women are supposed to behave.

A study by O'Sullivan and Byers (1992) asked unmarried, heterosexual college students to keep a record of their sexual activity during a 1-week period. Participants recorded whether sexual activity was initiated by themselves or their partner. An initiation was "any communication (verbal or nonverbal) by either partner of a desire to engage in sexual activity when no such behaviors were currently in progress" (O'Sullivan & Byers, 1992, p. 437). Sexual activity included a range of behaviors from kissing to sexual intercourse. Participants were also asked whether they had considered initiating sexual activity but did not do so. In 50% of the couples, both males and females initiated sex in the previous week. However, "only male" initiation of sexual activity (26%) was reported more frequently than "only female" initiation (7%). There was no difference between women and men in their likelihood of rejecting a sexual initiation by a partner.

When participants were asked if they considered initiating sex, there was no difference between men and women in the frequency that they had considered initiating sex but had not done so. The greater frequency of initiations by the males than females seemed to be due to couples following gender-based norms that males should initiate sexual activity. In the context of an ongoing relationship, there was no evidence, however, that females were more likely than males to play the restrictor role, perhaps because there are no "bad reputation" consequences of having sex with a steady partner.

There is evidence that when heterosexual couples are in a steady relationship, they are more likely to depart from traditional scripts that men should initiate the sexual encounter. There may be less risk of rejection for women initiating sex in a committed relationship (as well as for men to accept women's "advances") because sexual activity for women is considered more acceptable in intimate than in casual relationships (O'Sullivan & Byers, 1992). However, even in long-term relationships (including married and cohabiting individuals) male partners initiate sex more often than females partners do. For instance, Brown and Auerback (1981) examined patterns in initiation of sex among couples who had been married from 2 to 35 years. In the first year of marriage, men initiated sex about 75% of the time. In longer marriages, men still initiated sex 60% of the time. The fact that men more than women tend to initiate sex—even in stable relationships—indicates that traditional sexual scripts about males initiating sex still endure.

While gender is a powerful determinant of who initiates sexual activity among heterosexual couples, research indicates that gay and lesbian partners tend to take joint responsibility for initiating sex. Whereas gay men are more likely than lesbians to emphasize sex as a goal in dating (especially when going out with someone new), gay men and lesbians are equally likely to share responsibility with their partners about who initiates physical contact (Klinkenberg & Rose, 1994; Rose & Frieze, 1989). Because gay men and lesbians are not interacting with someone who plays a "traditional complementary, heterosexual role" (see Klinkenberg & Rose, 1994, p. 25), they are more likely than heterosexual men and women to coordinate sexual behavior based on their personal needs and desires.

We have emphasized how in heterosexual couples, men are more likely than women to initiate sexual activity. However, many males would be reluctant to, for example, approach a woman in a bar or lounge, ask a woman out for a date, or make an overt sexual move (such as touching a woman's breasts) unless she had already indicated some interest in him. As Perper and Weis (1987) have suggested, a sexual interaction may actually begin when women signal nonverbally their interest in a man and not when the man either asks the woman to have sex or makes a direct sexual move toward her. Women may control with whom and when they have sex by the use of so-called "proceptive behaviors" that indicate their interest in a man. For instance, in a dating bar, a woman might seek a man's attention by staring directly at him for a few seconds and then looking away quickly ("the short darting glance"), or she might smile, laugh, lean forward, whisper, toss her head, or hike her skirt briefly to attract his attention (see Moore, 1985).

Women may use proceptive cues to signal a man that they are willing to have sex with him. Perper and Weis (1987) asked women to describe how they would influence a man to have sex with them if they felt "really turned on by them." The accounts written by the college-age women emphasized the use of verbal and nonverbal signals to have the man "get the hint" that they were interested in having sex with him, and then he would "take it from there" to make an overt sexual gesture. Common proceptive strategies included moving close (the woman moves physically closer to the man or cuddles up to him), touching (holding hands, caressing his hair), or kissing. The woman might steer the conversation to talk about sexual or romantic feelings or she might dress in a way that is described as seductive or sexually arousing.

Here are illustrations of the proceptive strategies from Perper and Weis's (1987) study, strategies women reported using to signal their sexual interest:

> I attempt to influence the mood of my date by suggesting that we go somewhere quiet, relaxing, and secluded. . . . If my date likes this suggestion, I usually let him suggest the place in order to get a better idea of where his head is at. . . . If he asks for suggestions as to where to go, I inevitably suggest MY PLACE! (written by a 21-year-old woman, Perper & Weis, 1987, p. 468)

> Well, if I had known this person for 3 weeks and only dated him once in those 3 weeks, he may not be as attracted to me as I am to him, so it may take *some* influencing. . . . But then again, being a female, I don't believe the girl should make the first move . . . , since there has been no kind of sex between us yet. So if he's interested, he'll make a move. . . . If I wanted to influence this guy to kiss me . . . , I would probably sit close to him . . . as he talked to me . . . and smile a lot as he realizes that I am turned on and liked him a lot. (20-year-old woman, Perper & Weis, 1987, pp. 468-469)

> Move closer, start kissing, and take it from there. (18-year-old woman, Perper & Weis, 1987, p. 469)

These descriptions of proceptive behaviors describe how women can initiate a sexual encounter with a particular man by signaling their interest in him. As Perper and Weis (1987) note, "It is no longer adequate simply to say men push for sexual intimacy and women hesitate" (p. 474). On the other hand, the accounts also indicate that there is a give-and-take between partners as they signal and assess their interest and attraction for one another, via mutual eye contact, laughter, and conversation. Thus, both the female and male can "check out" a prospective sexual partner before any overt sexual act begins (Perper & Weis, 1987).

◆ Forced Sex

> My husband, Brent, is usually a good lover. What I don't like though is that he likes to pin me down when we have sex. This position makes me feel trapped and uncomfortable; sometimes, I even cry when he does it. When I complain, Brent usually stops and we do something else. But a couple of times when we had intercourse, he continued to hold me down when I asked him not to. I have told him that holding my hands down is unpleasant and that I can't enjoy sex if I am being forced to do something. (32-year-old married woman)

> I was 15. I had heard about rape. I knew I was supposed to be careful and not trust strangers, but nobody told me to be afraid of my date. . . . I didn't recognize it as rape at the time because he didn't hit me or yell at me; he just ignored me. He had sex with me while I was crying and saying no and asking, "Why are you doing this to me?" It was confusing. It happened so fast. (rape survivor, quoted in Muehlenhard, Julsonnet, Carlson, & Flarity-White, 1989, p. 211)

Couples may often misinterpret one another's interest in having sex. Usually, saying no to a particular sexual activity is enough to have the other person stop what they are doing. Sometimes, a partner (frequently a male) may not let a negative answer get in the way of his persisting to have sex. A recent survey of sexual behavior in the United States asked individuals whether after age 13 they had ever been forced to do something sexually that they did not want to do (Michael et al., 1994). The research found that 22% of the women reported having been forced to engage in some sexual activity that they did not want to do, whereas only 2% of the males had ever had a similar experience. In just about every case, the woman who had been forced to have sex was forced by a man. In one third of the cases where the man was forced to have sex, it was with another man. In examining the relationship of the women with the men who had forced them to engage in an unwanted sexual activity, Michael et al. (1994) found that in only 4% of the cases was the man a stranger. About 46% of the women reported being in love with the man who forced them to engage in unwanted sexual activity. About 22% reported knowing him well, 9% reported that the man was their spouse, and only 19% reported that the man was an acquaintance.

A U.S. national survey of the prevalence of sexual aggression experienced by women was conducted at colleges, universities, and technical schools by Koss and her colleagues (see Koss, Dinero, Seibel, & Cox, 1988; Koss, Gidycz, & Wisniewski, 1987). Sexual aggression was defined as the woman experiencing unwanted sexual activity because a man used force in some way. Females were asked if they had ever been forced to have sex with a man, and the males were asked if they had ever used force to induce a woman to have sex with them. Koss et al. (1987) found that 44% of the women had engaged in unwanted "sex play" such as kissing, petting, but not intercourse, because they had been overwhelmed by the man's arguments and verbal pressure; 25% of the women reported engaging in unwanted intercourse because of the man's arguments and verbal pressures. About 15% of the women in Koss et al.'s study could be classified as having been raped, meaning that some degree of physical force (such as twisting an arm, or holding the woman down) had been used to make her have sexual intercourse or to engage in other sexual acts (such as oral or anal penetration). Most men (75%) reported never having engaged in any form of sexual aggression, whereas 25% said they had been involved in some form of sexual aggression. Similar to other studies, rape victims in Koss's research were more likely to have been victimized by someone they knew than by a stranger. Most rapes occurred in a casual or steady dating situation (51%), 25% of rapes involved a nonromantic acquaintance (such as a friend, coworker, or neighbor), and 9% of rapes involved a husband or other family member (see Koss et al., 1988).

Why does forced sex (with women usually the victims) occur relatively often in dating relationships and among romantic partners? Let us review some possible explanations.

Gender-Related Sexual Scripts May Cause Misunderstandings About Sexual Intentions. Men are expected to take the initiative in asking for a date, driving the car, paying expenses on a date, and beginning explicit sexual advances. Women, even if they are interested in having sex, traditionally were not supposed to "give in to sex" too easily, or they were supposed to make some token resistance. Most men (perhaps after trying to persuade the woman to change her mind) stop when a woman says she doesn't want to engage in a certain activity. However, the male may misinterpret the message that the woman is trying to communicate. For instance, if a woman says she is not ready to have sex, the male may perceive her behavior as a token sign of resistance instead of a negative response. If the woman indicates her refusal indirectly (e.g., backing away physically, asking the man to stop touching her without explaining why) he might interpret her behavior as communicating sexual interest because she did not say no explicitly to having sex.

There is evidence that forced sex often occurs when males misinterpret women's intentions to have sex. That is, the man sees the woman as wanting some form of sexual activity when she means no. For instance, survey research indicates that whereas many women report having been pressured to do something sexually by a man, relatively few men report having forced a woman to have sex with them. In Michael et al.'s (1994) national survey of sexual behavior, only 3% of the men reported ever having forced a woman to have sex whereas almost 22% of the women said they had been forced to engage in sex, at some time with a man. In Koss et al.'s (1987) national survey of sexual aggression in colleges and technical schools in the United States, 54% of the women said they had been forced to engage in sexual behavior they did not want, but only 25% of the men admitted having engaged in sexually coercive behavior. In this study, 27.5% of women reported having experienced but only 7.7% of men reported having engaged in sexual acts that would meet legal definitions of rape. Also, males often feel "led on" in dates when forced sex occurs (Muehlenhard & Linton, 1987). It seems that males who force a woman physically or verbally to have sex may believe that the woman is consenting to engage in the sexual activity. As Koss et al. (1987) note, "It may be that some men fail to perceive accurately the degree of force and coerciveness that was involved in a particular sexual encounter or to interpret correctly a women's nonconsent and resistance" (p. 169).

Men May Have a Higher Overall Level of Sexual Interest Compared to Women. Males may have difficulty distinguishing when women are sexually interested in them versus just being friendly because they have a relatively "high base rate in sexual arousal" (Shotland & Craig, 1988, p. 72). Thus, some cases of sexual aggression engaged in by men may be partially due to their inability to distinguish when a woman is being friendly versus being sexually interested in him. Males are bombarded with advertisements and sexually graphic magazines depicting women as sexual objects. The disproportionate emphasis in American culture on women's sexual appeal may lead men to de-emphasize women's other qualities. Males may develop a *sexual gender schema* that causes them to see women's (and even men's) behavior as being sexually motivated (see Abbey, 1991). Also, males tend to have a relatively high level of "free testosterone" (which is associated with overall rate of sexual activity in males) when talking with a female (Dabbs, Ruback, & Besch, 1987). About 54% of males, compared to 19% of females, report that they think about sex every day or several times a day (Michael et al., 1994). Sexual arousal when interacting with a female may lead to males viewing women in terms of their sexual availability and, in some cases, assuming sexual interest on their part when none exists.

There is evidence that males compared to females are more likely to see the world through "sexual glasses" (Shotland & Craig, 1988, p. 66), which leads them to misinterpret the cues that women convey about being interested versus not being interested in having sex. For instance, Abbey (1982) designed a study in which pairs of males and females had a conversation with one another for 5 minutes. A pair of male and female observers were also assigned to watch the conversation from behind a one-way mirror. Abbey found that the males, either in the role of actors or observers, rated the female actor as being more promiscuous and seductive than did females. Males (whether in the role of actors or observers) also rated the male actor in a more sexualized way, rating the male actor as more flirtatious and seductive than the female subjects did. These results support the view that men may be more likely than women to see their world in sexual terms. If men perceive themselves and women as having a high interest in sex, males may be especially likely to misinterpret a woman's sexual interest no matter what she says or does.

Attitudes Toward Masculinity and Sexual Aggression. In just about every culture in the world, "manliness" and masculinity have been associated with having control and power as well as being aggressive (Gilmore, 1990). If traditional gender roles prescribe that men should take the first overt move to have sex, some men may believe that they should control what happens during the sexual interaction regardless of what the woman wants. Sexual aggression and rape may represent an "acting out" of characteristics that are thought to embody supermasculinity in many societies, such as being aggressive, forceful, tough, and dominant in interactions with others. Research conducted by Pleck, Sonnenstein, and Ku (1993a) among unmarried males between the ages of 15 and 19 found that the willingness to endorse traditional attitudes about the male role was associated with the use of forced sex. Males who scored high on a measure of *masculinity ideology* (emphasizing the importance of a man being respected by others, being tough, and not acting like a girl) were more likely to say they had tricked or forced someone else to have sex with them. Thus, the pressure that males feel to prove their masculinity via sexual performance may contribute to their being sexually aggressive and coercive in dating and romantic relationships.

❧ Conclusions

Perhaps being a "good lover to your partner" and "keeping the excitement of sex alive" in a committed relationship require that we free ourselves from traditional societal views of how men and women should behave sexually. As individuals, men *and* women must take more direct responsibility for communicating what they want or desire sexually instead of relying on gender-based rules of what they can and cannot say or do.

Consider the following example: In June 1992, Antioch College in Ohio passed a set of rules governing sexual interactions among students. Individuals must ask their partner's verbal consent before initiating a new level of sexual intimacy. Individuals cannot take silence as consent for beginning a sexual activity. The other person must say, for instance, "Yes, I want you to do it." While some may think it is boorish or silly to communicate directly with their sexual partner about what they want sexually, assigning both genders the responsibility for stating what they want may discourage misunderstandings and ensure that partners are attentive to one another's desires (Antioch College, 1992).

Sex per se is not a simple act. Although sex may be physically and emotionally satisfying, sex also serves other goals, such as confirming one's sense of masculinity or femininity and fulfilling social expectations about how "males" and "females" ought to behave. A major feature of having a good sexual relationship is being sensitive to your own and your partner's needs and desires. Our goal here has been to show how gender-based rules and expectations influence and sometimes get in the way of males and females being equal sexual partners.

4

Relationship Maintenance

W hat happens in a relationship after it has begun? Does it glide along smoothly at whatever level it reached in the beginning? Does a sort of gravitational force pull it inevitably down, so that happy newlyweds become dissatisfied couples? Does it go up and down like a roller coaster? What differences do children make?

Although the beginnings and endings have attracted more attention from relationship researchers, there is growing research literature on *maintenance*, the keeping of relationships. Certainly it is this in-between period that most of us are "in." Starting new relationships or ending relationships may involve more drama and emotion and even be more memorable, but we spend most of our time keeping the relationships we have. How do we do this, and how does gender influence the process of maintaining relationships?

This chapter will review the literature on gender and maintenance. Do women or men do more to maintain relationships? Assuming that relationship satisfaction and stability are markers of a "maintained" relationship, this chapter will also examine the literature on predictors of relationship satisfaction and stability and the effects of gender on these predictors. Finally, in addition to the interpersonal work done to maintain relationships, being a couple also requires household work: domestic chores, such as cleaning, cooking, and shopping, money management, and work on the house, yard, and car. How do couples divide up this work? And, what is the impact of children on adult partnerships and the division of labor in families?

⁓ Maintenance Behaviors

The first question that relationship researchers have wanted to answer about relationship maintenance is: What do people actually *do* in order to maintain a relationship? Attempts to establish lists of maintenance behaviors have involved asking participants to rate behaviors derived from examination of existing research as well as asking participants to come up with their own lists of behaviors. A compilation of the lists from studies focusing on romantic, dating, or marital relationships (Dainton & Stafford, 1993; Dindia, 1994; Dindia & Baxter, 1987; Stafford & Canary, 1991) includes:

1. Being positive and cheerful
2. Being open, self-disclosing; talking about the relationship
3. Giving assurances, demonstrating love and faithfulness
4. Spending time with friends and family
5. Sharing tasks
6. Doing activities together
7. Sending cards, calling
8. Expressing affection, being sexually intimate
9. Engaging in celebrations and rituals
10. Being spontaneous
11. Avoiding or ignoring problematic issues/behaviors

Partners may engage in these activities intentionally in order to maintain a positive relationship, or the activity may be so routine that its relationship-promoting qualities are not conscious or deliberate. It may well be that, whereas partners are aware of maintenance behaviors in the first stages of a relationship, as the relationship continues, these behaviors become routine. In fact, Dindia and Baxter (1987) found that participants who had been married longer listed fewer maintenance behaviors than those who had been in a relationship for a shorter period of time.

If we ask partners about their maintenance behaviors, are there differences between women and men? When asked to list maintenance strategies, women and men list the same number (Dindia & Baxter, 1987), and they sort them into categories in similar ways (Baxter & Dindia, 1990), suggesting that women and men view maintenance of relationships in much the same way.

In a balanced relationship, we would expect both partners to engage in equal numbers and types of maintenance activities. But we often hear that women do more than 50% to maintain and nurture relationships. Is this true? When asked to what extent they or their partners engage in these behaviors, findings are mixed. Some data indicate that in the early stages of romantic relationships, it is actually men who do more to maintain the relationship, by talking about it and trying to resolve problems (Huston, Surra, Fitzgerald, & Cate, 1981) and by spending time thinking about it (Burnett, 1987), whereas later in the relationships, these same researchers found that women spend more time and effort than men on these maintenance activities. Examining a wider range of maintenance behaviors across four stages of relationship development (dating, seriously dating, engaged, and married) Stafford and Canary (1991) did not find that sex differences varied with stage of relationship. They did find, however, that women reported more maintenance behaviors from their male partners than men reported from their female partners. The specific behaviors that women felt their partners provided more of were being positive (e.g., nice, cheerful, romantic, patient, cooperative), giving assurances, and spending time with friends. A difference between this and the other studies is that participants reported on their partners' behaviors as well as their own. In another study, including only husbands and wives, Canary and Stafford (1992) found that wives reported more openness, sharing tasks, and spending time with friends than husbands did and that, in reporting on their partners' maintenance behaviors, wives reported less openness and sharing of tasks from husbands than husbands reported from wives. Finally, Dainton and Stafford (1993) studied married and dating partners. They found that in the dating group, women were more likely than men to report expressing affection and, in the married group, women were more likely than men to report being positive, being open, talking ("verbal communication that is not as deep as openness"), and avoiding problematic topics/behavior. They conclude that women may, in fact, do more to maintain relationships than men do. Given the differences in number of gender differences between dating and married couples, and consistent with the work of Huston et al. (1981) and Burnett (1987), it may be that over time, women come to assume more of the relationship maintenance responsibilities.

These studies have obtained results for positive maintenance behaviors. What about the things couples do to hold onto a relationship when things are not going so well? In a sample of 51 couples, married an average of 8 years, Hendrick (1981) found that both husbands and wives blamed more marriage problems on wives. Hendrick (1981) argues that this may reflect wives' assuming responsibility for maintaining the relationship. It may also reflect women's and men's customary responses to relationship problems, with women wanting to talk about them and men seeking to avoid them (see Chapter 5). Supporting this interpretation are the results of work by Rusbult (1987), who has described four basic responses to relationship conflict: loyalty (remaining committed without actively doing anything to resolve the conflict), voice (encouraging conflict resolution in a positive way), neglect (avoiding conflict and hoping it will go away), and exit (leaving the relationship). Rusbult (1987) reports that women, both heterosexual and lesbian, are more likely to use loyalty or voice responses to relationship problems, whereas men, both heterosexual and gay, are more likely to use neglect or exit. Women appear to be more willing to engage their partners even when there are problems and even at the expense of being seen as blameworthy.

Women's and men's responses to conflict may also depend on the current state of the relationship. In a laboratory study, Gottman, Markman, and Notarius (1977) had distressed and non-distressed married couples engage in a discussion of a relationship problem, and the interaction was videotaped. They found that distressed husbands and wives and nondistressed husbands were highly likely to become negative speakers if their spouse displayed negative affect. In other words, negativity was reciprocated. But nondistressed wives were less likely to respond negatively, thus potentially breaking a negative cycle of exchanges. On the other hand, distressed wives, compared to nondistressed wives and nondistressed and distressed husbands, were especially unlikely to respond with a positive response to a negative message from husbands (Notarius, Benson, Sloane, Vanzetti, & Hornyak, 1989). Taken together, these results suggest that in nondistressed couples, wives are the ones who act to interrupt a negative exchange, but in distressed couples, wives are the ones who are unwilling to insert positive comments in a negative exchange. Gottman and Levenson (1992) state,

> Our observations of hundreds of marital interactions over the years has led us to hypothesize that wives are much more likely than husbands to take responsibility for regulating the affective balance in a marriage and for keeping the couple focused on the problem-solving task during the problem-area marital interaction. (p. 232)

Do maintenance behaviors generally make for better relationships? Stafford and Canary (1991) found moderate to strong relationships between maintenance behaviors and mutuality, liking, commitment, and satisfaction, and Kelly, Huston, and Cate (1985) found maintenance to be associated with feelings of love and negatively related to ambivalence. So the answer seems to be a definite yes. This is hardly surprising. We would probably all agree for the most part that these maintenance behaviors are the ingredients of a happy and satisfying relationship. But are there somewhat different contributors to relationship satisfaction for women than for men?

๛ Predicting Relationship Satisfaction and Stability

Louise and Mark just celebrated their 10th wedding anniversary. They consider their relationship to be stable and satisfying most of the time. Louise feels that Mark avoids discussions of the problems they do have, and she still wishes he would talk to her more about how he feels about her and the relationship. Mark thinks everything is just fine; what is there to discuss? They have postponed having children. Louise has gotten her master's degree, and Mark has been doing well in his career.

There are several theories about how relationships work, and an important ingredient in some of these theories is our expectations about what a relationship should be. If women and men have different expectations about relationships, then they may well be affected differently in terms of what makes a relationship satisfying and enduring. Helgeson, Shaver, and Dyer (1987) asked male and female undergraduates to describe times when they felt intimate with and distant from a same-sex and an opposite-sex person. Every behavior, feeling, and thought in the participants' descriptions was categorized, and cluster analyses were done to compare female versus male and same- versus opposite-sex descriptions of intimacy and distance. For intimacy with an opposite-sex partner, the results indicated that sex and physical contact formed a separate component for males but not for females. Women rarely mentioned sex (sex was mentioned seven times more often by men), and in the women's data, physical contact was grouped with feeling and expressing appreciation and enjoyment. *Having* positive feelings about one's intimate partner was mentioned by almost all female and male respondents. *Expressing* those feelings, however, was mentioned significantly more often by women than by men. Both men and women also mentioned talking and sharing activities in their descriptions of intimacy. Talking was mentioned more often than activity sharing, but there were no sex differences in either of these variables in descriptions of intimacy. (See Chapter 6 on friendships for a discussion of descriptions of same-sex intimacy.) Participants also reported feelings of apprehension in their descriptions of intimacy. These apprehensive feelings were related to sex in the men's accounts of intimacy and to expressing appreciation in the women's accounts.

Gender differences in accounts of intimacy in opposite-sex relationships suggest that sex is more important for males and expressions of affection for females. Karney and Bradbury (1995), however, found that in longitudinal studies of marital stability and satisfaction, sexual satisfaction was a positive predictor for both females and males, with virtually no difference in power of prediction. The fact that men describe intimacy in terms of sex whereas women do not, but that men's and women's relationships are equally positively affected by satisfying sex, may reflect a double standard in terms of who has permission to talk freely about sex. Women may censor their thoughts about sex, even in intimate relationships, in order to avoid being considered promiscuous.

Consistent with women's emphasis on expressions of affection in intimate relationships, some authors have concluded that marital satisfaction is more dependent on the husband's than the wife's expressiveness. Social support from husbands predicts wives' general well-being and marital satisfaction in older couples (Acitelli & Antonucci, 1994) and wives' marital satisfaction in young to midlife couples (Julien & Markman, 1991); social support from wives is a weak or nonsignificant predictor of husbands' satisfaction in these studies. Acitelli (1992) found that the degree to which husbands talk about their marital relationship was positively related to their wives' marital well-being, but wives' talk was not related to husbands' marital well-being. Vannoy-Hiller and Philliber (1989) report that husband's sensitivity predicts the wife's marital quality, but the wife's sensitivity has no influence on husband's marital quality. These studies suggest that women are more satisfied with male partners who are expressive in the relationship; whereas males are relatively unaffected by their partner's level of expressiveness.

Helgeson et al. (1987) also had participants describe an experience of distance with a same- and opposite-sex partner. Distance was conceptualized primarily as feelings of disapproval of the partner's behavior. Women described themselves and their partners feeling hurt more often than men did, and females also mentioned feeling awkward, whereas males did not. Men mentioned arguing more often than women did and said that their female partner complied or gave in more often (Helgeson et al., 1987). In general, women seem to think of distance in an opposite-sex relationship in terms of hurt and discomfort, whereas men think of it in terms of conflict. In line with these gender differences in accounts of distance in opposite-sex relationships, Gottman and Levenson (1986) found that, in a conflictual discussion between husbands and wives, 78% of the husbands' expressions of negative affect were anger and contempt, whereas 93% of the wives' expressions of negative affect were fear, sadness, and complaining. For a thorough discussion of gender and conflict in relationships, see Chapter 5.

A limitation of the Helgeson et al. (1987) study is that the participants were undergraduates, whereas most work on relationship maintenance focuses on marriage or at least serious dating relationships. Nevertheless, their study suggests some gender differences in the beliefs and assumptions about intimacy and distance with which individuals enter heterosexual relationships.

Another source of expectations about relationships is gender stereotypes. We believe that women are relationship-oriented and more likely than men to care about relationships and to work to maintain them, and that men are independent and reluctant to commit. Indeed, a problem with the psychological data that tend to confirm these stereotypes is that to the extent they are obtained through self-report, they may be a reflection of the stereotype rather than true behavioral differences between women and men. (Fortunately some data, such as the ratings of videotaped interactions and studies of whether couples stay together or split up/get divorced, are not obtained through self-report.) However, if these are the relationship behaviors we expect from women and men, those individuals who do not conform to the stereotypes may pay a price.

The results of a longitudinal study by Kirkpatrick and Davis (1994) demonstrate this possibility. They were studying the stability of relationships in which individuals had different attachment styles: secure, anxious, or avoidant. Secure individuals are those who are comfortable with closeness. Anxious individuals are also referred to as ambivalent and preoccupied; they are eager for relationships but concerned about abandonment. Avoidant individuals are those who fear relationships and keep their distance. Certainly the anxious attachment style is closer to the female relationship stereotype, and the avoidant attachment style is closer to the male relationship stereotype. Kirkpatrick and Davis (1994) recruited undergraduate participants who were in steady or serious dating relationships. They gathered data on the attachment style of each partner, and in two follow-up telephone interviews (7 to 14 months later and 30 to 36 months later), they assessed the stability of the relationship. About 75% of the participants, female and male, described themselves as secure. Of particular interest, however, are the outcomes for avoidant and anxious women and men. Although avoidant men had the lowest levels of relationship satisfaction at Time 1, they had high relationship stability. The anxious men displayed the lowest level of stability. At Time 3 the relationships of anxious women were significantly more stable (70%) than those of avoidant women (35%), with secure women (51%) in between. Thus, the anxious women and the avoidant men, those fitting the gender stereotypes, had surprisingly high relationship stability. The avoidant women and the anxious men, those with counterstereotypical relationship styles, had the lowest levels of relationship stability. Perhaps partners of avoidant men or anxious women find their partners' behaviors acceptable, although not ideal, because of their beliefs about men and women in general (she worries about the relationship all the time; he's unwilling to commit—"That's just the way women (or men) are"). But partners of avoidant women or anxious men may consider their behavior to be peculiar and unacceptable (he worries about the relationship all the time; she's unwilling to commit—"What's wrong with him [or her]?").

Most studies of relationship satisfaction have focused on heterosexual dating or marital relationships. Gay and lesbian couples also vary in terms of relationship satisfaction and stability. In a series of studies of cohabiting gay and lesbian couples, Kurdek (1989, 1991a, 1991b, 1995) has examined predictors of relationship satisfaction and dissolution. It might be argued that relationships between two men or two women would be most likely to demonstrate differences that gender has on relationship functioning. Indeed, Kurdek found that compared to gay couples, lesbian couples had higher scores on ideal levels of equality in a relationship (Kurdek, 1995), reported higher levels of relationship satisfaction and liking of partner (Kurdek, 1989), and reported more rewards from their relationship (Kurdek, 1991a). When variables that predict relationship satisfaction or stability are examined, however, there are no differences between gay and lesbian couples (Kurdek, 1989, 1995). Factors such as shared decision making, strong trust, and satisfaction with social support predict relationship satisfaction (Kurdek, 1989), and similarity in actual and ideal levels of equality and balance between perceived levels of attachment and autonomy predict relationship commitment (Kurdek, 1995) for both gay and lesbian couples. Reasons given for ending a relationship and reactions to its dissolution were also similar for gay and lesbian couples (Kurdek, 1991b).

These studies rely on self-reports. Participants fill out scales that describe their relationships and their feelings about the relationship. A danger in looking at gender differences in self-report questionnaires is that our own gender stereotypes may affect our responses to self-report measures. To say that relationships are rewarding or satisfying may be something that is easier for women than for men.

One way around relying on self-reports is bringing couples into the laboratory, videotaping their interactions, and then having trained observers rate their behavior. Perhaps reflecting a research bias, studies of this sort have been done extensively only with heterosexual married couples. But they have yielded interesting results in terms of what predicts a decline in relationship satisfaction over time. Husbands who feel less positive in low-conflict situations and less negative in high-conflict situations (Levenson & Gottman, 1985) and display less disagreement and criticism in high-conflict situations (Gottman & Krokoff, 1989) but are more likely to reciprocate wives' negative behavior (Julien, Markman, & Lindahl, 1989) are those headed for an unhappy relationship. These behaviors have been interpreted as representing husbands' efforts to avoid conflict or disengage when there is a relationship problem. Wives' behaviors that predict declines in relationship satisfaction include feeling more positive in low-conflict situations (Levenson & Gottman, 1985), being more likely to reciprocate husband's positive behavior in high-conflict situations (Julien et al., 1989), and being more agreeing and approving of husbands and showing more sadness in high-conflict situations (Gottman & Krokoff, 1989). The generally positive behaviors by wives in relationships that become less satisfying over time suggest that women are trying to maintain the relationship even as its quality declines.

If asked what makes a relationship work, most people would probably come up with very similar lists. They would probably mention various positive behaviors, such as respect, caring, good communication, responsiveness, and agreeableness. They might think of other factors, such as similarity between partners in attitudes or personality and sexual satisfaction. Demographic variables, such as age, education, and income or employment, are often mentioned, especially in terms of warnings: "Don't commit when you are too young" or "Finish your education before you get involved." If these are the variables that make relationships work, shouldn't they affect females and males in similar ways? In a review of 115 longitudinal studies of marital quality and stability, Karney and Bradbury (1995) report (1) that agreeableness, conscientiousness, positive behavior, similarity in personality and attitudes, being older, and having more education *do* predict relationship satisfaction and/or stability, and (2) there are few gender differences in what predicts marital satisfaction or stability when all effects are taken into account. (No measures of interpersonal or communication skill, however, are included in the results.) One dramatic exception to the lack of gender differences is that husband's positive behavior predicts more marital satisfaction over time ($r = +.54$) (an understandable finding), whereas wife's positive behavior predicts *less* marital satisfaction over time ($r = -.43$). As discussed above, it may be that women increase their positive behaviors in an effort to save a declining relationship.

Another well-substantiated exception is the influence of employment. Husbands' employment has positive effects on the marriage (stability and satisfaction), for both husbands and wives, but wives' employment has a slight negative effect on marital stability (there are no data reported for marital satisfaction) (Karney & Bradbury, 1995). Marital satisfaction has been found to suffer when a wife's salary becomes greater than her husband's (Philliber & Hiller, 1979), a condition that also increases the likelihood of divorce (Trent & South, 1989).

As these outcomes suggest, maintenance of relationships occurs in a larger context. People in relationships do or do not work outside the home. Shared living space must be cared for. Daily tasks, such as food preparation, housework, and keeping up relations with family and friends, must be attended to. Who does these tasks, and how do these activities influence relationship maintenance?

⮞ Division of Labor

Five years later, Mark and Louise have two small children. Before the children were born, the couple divided the work around the house pretty evenly. If one person cooked dinner, the other person cleaned up. They kept a list of things needed at the store and tried to make sure that both of them did the shopping. Louise did worry more about keeping the house clean. After little Alice and John were born, Louise took maternity leave. There was a lot more to do around the house and in terms of errands (e.g., visits to the doctor, buying diapers, arranging play groups, and arranging for day care). Louise did more of these things and felt responsible for seeing that they got done. Even though Louise went back to work, Mark felt responsible for providing financial security and setting money aside for the children's college and other expenses.

The woman cares for home and children; the man is the bread-winner. Is this the pattern your grandparents followed? Your parents? Are you in a relationship like this now, or do you think you ever will be? What if the woman works outside the home? Does that make her a breadwinner? Who does the family work when both partners are employed?

Before reviewing the research on division of labor and its effects on relationships, it is useful to consider: What *is* the labor that goes into caring for a home? You might make a list of all the things you can think of that need to be done to keep a household running. Among the items on the list would be cooking, cleaning, laundry, yardwork, repairs, finances (e.g., paying bills), and car maintenance. What about pets? Did you think of shopping? Eating requires lots of grocery shopping as well as food preparation. But items for the home also need to be purchased. These things may keep the home and its occupants going, but what about other things that couples need to do, such as entertaining friends and staying in touch with family and remembering birthdays? And what happens when a couple has children (as 90% of them do)? Children require feeding, clothing, supervising, playing with, help with homework, chauffeuring, arranging care for children when parents are not home, organizing activities with friends, shopping for clothes, school supplies, and so on, and lots more. All of these together have been referred to as family work and, as you can see, it's a big job. Who does it? And in addition to who *does* the tasks, who is *responsible*? It is one thing to have someone say, "Honey, please clean the bathroom" and then do it. It is another to be in charge of making sure the bathroom is clean, whether you do it yourself or get someone else to do it.

If you are a young adult in a relationship, especially if you are both working or going to school, you might respond to these questions with "We both do stuff; it's only fair." You might want to try answering the items in Table 4.1 and see if it's true that you share chores or, if not, who does more.

Most adults value equity in relationships and, if both partners are busy with school and work, then they believe both should pitch in when it comes to housework. Most college students we talk to agree with this, often say this is true in their current

Table 4.1 Measuring Who Does Family Work

Use the scale below to indicate the level of involvement of both you and your partner. Consider the amount of work done by you and your partner only. If you do not have children, answer items 1 to 12; if you have children, answer all 26 items. Do not consider work done by someone else in the household or by outside help.

I do almost entirely 1	*I do more than my partner* 2	*My partner and I do about the same* 3	*My partner does more than I* 4	*My partner does almost entirely* 5	*Does not apply* 6

1.	_____	Grocery shopping
2.	_____	Meal preparation
3.	_____	Clean house
4.	_____	Laundry
5.	_____	General repairs to house
6.	_____	Meal clean-up
7.	_____	Yard work
8.	_____	Car maintenance and repairs
9.	_____	Pay bills
10.	_____	Make major purchases
11.	_____	Make investments
12.	_____	Shop for household items
13.	_____	Attend child's activities
14.	_____	Take child to the doctor
15.	_____	Attend child's teacher conference
16.	_____	Supervise child's morning routine
17.	_____	Pick up/clean child's room
18.	_____	Spend time at bedtime with child
19.	_____	Take child to or from school
20.	_____	Buy child's clothes
21.	_____	Take child on outing (e.g., museum, movie, park)
22.	_____	Give or supervise child's bath
23.	_____	Discipline child
24.	_____	Talk with child about concerns
25.	_____	Arrange babysitting/childcare
26.	_____	Supervise child's homework

SOURCE: From *Causal Models of Work-Family Conflict from Family and Organizational Perspectives*, by Lyse Guttau Wells, 1996; unpublished doctoral dissertation, Old Dominion University. Reprinted by permission of the author.

relationship, and seem to believe it will always be this way. But studies show clearly that the arrival of children "traditionalizes" family work (Belsky, 1990; MacDermid, Huston, & McHale, 1990). That is, when a couple has children, women assume the majority of the responsibility for child care and often other family work as well. There are many possible reasons for this. In the weeks and months following the birth of a child, the mother and father must adapt to her/his needs. Nearly always, it is the mother who takes leave from work (fathers often do not even have the opportunity to take parental leave), and so she becomes accustomed to doing the child care and actually acquires skills that the father may not have the opportunity to develop. Being at home, even for a limited period of time, she may also assume greater responsibility for other household tasks. If she cuts back on out-of-home work, she may be expected to do more in-home tasks. The neglect of certain household work (e.g., not grocery shopping because you can always go out to eat, not cleaning because no harm can come to anyone from having stuff strewn everywhere) is no longer possible. A lifestyle that supported an equal division of domestic work has changed.

If a man is employed full-time and his partner, who is not employed outside the home because she wishes to stay home with the children, does the family work or most of it, this arrangement may be seen as fair. Basically, one partner does one type of job (income earning) and the other does another (family work). We often refer to this as the traditional couple or family. This arrangement can serve the purposes of both partners, as long as the couple stays together. Unfortunately, when a traditional couple separates or divorces, the woman has no source of income, other than what her ex-partner is willing or required to provide, and she is at a disadvantage when she tries to reenter the job market because of her lack of employment experience.

In the 1990s, however, there are relatively few traditional couples. For economic and personal reasons, most women in relationships, including women with children, work outside the home. The fair exchange of income for family work no longer applies. In fact, a 1989 Gallup poll found that most adults (57%) believe that the ideal marriage is one in which both partners have jobs and share family work (DeStefano & Colasanto, 1990, reported in Steil, 1994). But what sort of arrangements do couples actually make today? It is clear that women still do much more family work than men, 65% to 72% according to recent studies (Blair & Lichter, 1991; Blumstein & Schwartz, 1991). Even when both people in a couple work full-time outside the home, only 2% to 20% of couples share equally in family work (Ferree, 1991; Hochschild, 1989). Hochschild (1989) refers to the work that women do after a day of working outside the home as the "second shift." Trends show that men *are* participating more in family work. Perhaps as women's participation in the labor force becomes the norm, gender roles are changing. Still, women are doing more than men.

To look at what happens when wives and husbands with young children are both pursuing a demanding career and raising a family, Biernat and Wortman (1991) recruited a sample of 139 married couples in which the wife was a business executive or a university professor. Husbands were older and made somewhat more than their wives. Businesswomen reported spending significantly more hours on the job than any other group, but the female professors reported significantly higher job involvement than any other group. Reports of child care and household chores, however, indicated that wives did significantly more to care for children and home and that they were more concerned about problems around the house. Biernat and Wortman (1991) concluded that despite equality in terms of career involvement, they "discovered substantial inequity within the home, particularly in the distribution of child-care tasks and the overall responsibility for seeing that tasks get done" (p. 855).

Fish, New, and Van Cleave (1992) identified a sample of dual-income couples who reported that they shared child care equally. There were no differences between husbands and wives in number of hours worked outside the home or in income. Of 15 identified child care tasks, women and men did not differ on 11 of them, which is hardly surprising because the couples were selected specifically because they said they shared child care. Women, however, did significantly more food preparation, care during illness, and shopping for the child, whereas men did more playing with the child. On the 15 household tasks, women and men differed on 9 of them. Women did more cooking, grocery shopping, laundry, and sewing; men did more car maintenance, car repair, financial investment, taking out garbage, and yardwork. In this case, men actually are responsible for more tasks (5) than women (4). The dividing of household chores into hers versus his along the line of inside versus outside tasks is common. Researchers have pointed out, however, that those tasks that women generally assume are more frequent (cooking has to be done for three meals a day, whereas cars may not need attention very often, and yard-work is seasonal), more time-consuming (vacuuming takes longer than taking out garbage), and not discretionary (groceries and laundry can wait only so long, whereas an unwashed car still runs—not so, of course, for a car that needs repairs—and financial investments can be done in spare time). Ferree (1987) estimates that the stereotypical male tasks make up about 20% of the total housework. Fish et al. (1992) also asked couples who took responsibility for maintaining their own relationship and maintaining relationships with family and friends. Women took a significantly greater proportion of the responsibility for all three. Despite these differences, 95% of the men and 94% of the women reported that they felt they had egalitarian marriages. In truth, these couples are probably about as close to egalitarian as couples come in terms of being equally engaged in paid work and nearly equally engaged in child care. Even so, household tasks are divided in gender stereotypical ways, and women take proportionately more responsibility for more time-consuming tasks and for main-tenance of relationships, both within and outside the family.

Studies of family work agree that women do more, despite their work hours outside the home or their income. Of course, it does make a difference if women are employed. Employed wives do less housework than unemployed wives, but husbands of employed wives do only a little more than husbands of un-employed wives (Ferree, 1991; Pleck, 1985). Husbands of employed wives tend to increase the time they spend on child care, although as seen above, certain aspects of child care remain a woman's job. One factor that may contribute to these inequalities is that husbands and wives tend to see the wife's job as less important than the husband's, even when she earns more than he does. Believing that her career *is* important can make a difference.

The best predictor of equality in family work among dual-career couples was how important a wife said her career was relative to her husband's career (Steil & Weltman, 1990).

How do partners view the division of labor? In their study of professional women and their husbands described above, Biernat and Wortman (1991) found that only 25% thought their husbands did too little, 62% said their husbands did a satisfactory amount, and 14% said their husbands did too much. Hochschild (1989), who labeled family work the second shift, found that even though only 18% of men shared this second shift equally with their wives, most women did not actively try to change the division of labor. Social scientists have generally been puzzled by the fact that the distribution of family work appears to be clearly inequitable but women do not seem especially unhappy about this fact. Thompson (1991) and Major (1993) have sought to explain why women appear satisfied with an unfair division of labor. Thompson (1991) suggests that women may evaluate their husband's contributions by his willingness to do disliked tasks, to give them some personal time, and to help out rather than by his equal participation in family work. Thompson (1991) and Major (1993) both suggest that women make comparisons between their situation and that of others. If they see that their husbands do more than their neighbor's husband or more than their own fathers, they may be satisfied. Hochschild (1989) found that women were more likely to compare themselves to other women, often favorably, rather than to their husband, which might lead to an unfavorable outcome. She describes women who shifted their standard of comparison from their partners to same-sex others, perhaps to avoid feeling unfairly treated. Both Thompson (1991) and Major (1993) also review justifications made for the inequitable division of labor. Women and men may believe that women are more skilled at domestic and child care tasks and therefore have an easier time doing them. If a woman expresses more concern about cleanliness around the house, she may be told, "It looks fine to me, but if it bothers you, clean it." Even when women work full-time outside the home and contribute a substantial portion of the family income, *responsibility* for the breadwinner role may still be assigned to the man, leaving the woman more responsible for the family work role. In fact, Blumstein and Schwartz (1983) found that when either partner views the male as the provider, the husband is more powerful regardless of his partner's income. Having more power may also allow men to "get out of" the unpleasant chores that are a part of family work.

How does division of labor affect marital satisfaction? There is some evidence that a more traditional division of labor (wife does more) benefits husbands and makes wives less satisfied (White, Booth, & Edwards, 1986). Many studies have found that wives are happier or more satisfied when husbands share family work (Barnett & Baruch, 1987; Hochschild, 1989). Vannoy-Hiller and Philliber (1989) found that both husbands and wives reported greater marital quality when the husband participated more in family work. But Crouter, Perry-Jenkins, Huston, and McHale (1987) found that father's involvement in child care was related to less love of his wife and more negative marital interactions. Often it is the *perception* of the division of labor that has been found to have an impact on marital quality. Pina and Bengtson (1993) found that a wife's satisfaction with the help and support she receives from her husband predicts her perceptions of positive interaction, closeness, and affirmation in her marriage. Perry-Jenkins and Folk (1994) reported a positive link between wives' perceptions of fairness in division of labor and their marital satisfaction. Perceptions of fairness did not predict husbands' marital satisfaction, however.

Some studies have found that the presence of children in the home is related to lower marital satisfaction (Belsky, 1990, reviews these studies). Two studies (Grote, Frieze, & Stone, 1996; White et al., 1986) have shown that it is the traditional division of family work that accounts for wives' dissatisfaction. Grote et al. (1996) did not find a relationship between number of children and men's marital satisfaction. They also found that the more family work men reported doing, the less satisfied they were with their marriage. They conclude,

> A striking feature of our results is that married men and women in our study appear to be caught in a Catch-22 situation—the dilemma is that one spouse's gain in love and marital satisfaction may be the

other's loss, unless perhaps a perceived balanced division of labor is achieved. Unfortunately, the married women in this sample do not experience the positive effects on love of the sharing of family tasks because they . . . do the lion's share of the family work. Conversely, this traditional domestic arrangement seems to have a beneficial effect on men's marital quality. (Grote et al., 1996, p. 225)

Although the benefits of sharing family work seem clear for women, the findings for men are mixed. Sharing for men probably means doing more than other men they know and more than their fathers. As one husband/father said to his wife: "If I compare myself to you (wife), I'm not doing enough; but if I compare myself to other men, I think I'm doing *a lot.*"

In heterosexual couples, the division of labor is clearly dictated by gender. How do lesbian and gay couples handle these tasks? Kurdek (1993) studied gay, lesbian, and heterosexual married couples to answer this question. Examining only domestic chores, those most frequently done by women, he found that heterosexual couples allocated these tasks to women, gay men divided tasks equitably (one partner did some things, the other partner did others), and lesbians tended, significantly more than the other two groups, to share domestic tasks (both partners did them). These findings reflect others that demonstrate the high value that lesbians place on sharing and equality. Kurdek (1993) also examined the relationship between doing these tasks and various other participant characteristics. He found that doing more domestic tasks was related to depression and global distress in women in heterosexual marriages, although not to less relationship satisfaction. Nor was doing more domestic tasks related to marital satisfaction for heterosexual men or gay partners. For the lesbian partners, however, doing more domestic chores was positively related to relationship satisfaction and to *less* depression and *less* global distress. Because household labor has generally been considered to be drudgery, Kurdek (1993) concludes,

It is unlikely that lesbian partners actually enjoy household labor more than wives. However, it is likely that lesbian partners performed household labor because they chose to do it, unlike wives who did household labor because they felt resigned to do it. (p. 138)

ⅷ Conclusions

What have we learned about the work that women and men do to maintain their intimate relationships? As has been the case in other chapters, we find that the stereotype of the woman who does more than her share of the relationship work has some truth, but is not as clear-cut as we might have thought. Men may actually do more at the beginning of a relationship, which is congruent with their role as the relationship initiator. Later, as couples settle into their relationship routines, it seems that women pick up more of the relationship maintenance activities.

In terms of what makes for a stable and satisfying relationship for men and women, there are relatively few differences. Men or women who do not fit their relationship stereotype (e.g., men who are anxious and preoccupied about relationships or women who avoid relationships) may have less stable relationships. Women's relationships seem to be positively influenced more by having a sensitive, expressive partner than men's relationships are. But sexual satisfaction is no better a predictor for men than for women. Gay men and lesbians, for whom gender differences might be expected to be exaggerated, also show similar patterns in terms of what predicts satisfaction and stability. Finally, in problematic relationships, men tend to withdraw and women to engage, exhibiting positive behaviors in relationships that become less satisfying over time.

Only for the more concrete side of maintenance, family work, is there clear evidence that women do more than men. In this chapter, we focused on studies that investigated patterns of family work in couples where both work equal numbers of hours outside the home. These provide the most indisputable evidence that women do more of the second shift. The continuing assumption that males should be the breadwinner, even in families where women contribute half of the income, may give men the power and opportunity to avoid many aspects of family work. Interestingly, Kurdek (1993) found that for lesbian partners, who were more likely than heterosexual or gay partners to share domestic chores, doing these chores did not appear to be drudgery because it was correlated with relationship satisfaction and less depression or global distress. Maybe family work is more rewarding when it is shared and not obligatory.

As we as a society place more value on intact families and see that relationships, although fragile, are worth the effort it takes to maintain them, and as more women and men see women's jobs or careers as important contributions to the family, we may find a move toward even greater gender equality in relationship maintenance activities.

5

Conflict and Violence

As partners in a relationship become more intimate, there is more potential for conflict. Conflicts may arise based on differences in assumptions about partners' roles in the relationship (e.g., how should couples divide housekeeping chores, how much autonomy should partners have in interacting with others beyond the relationship). Conflicts may occur about how to communicate as couples try to cope with disagreements (e.g., one partner may prefer to talk about the difficulty, whereas the other wants to avoid talking; one partner may express feelings of anger and annoyance, whereas the other wants to talk "rationally").

Although conflicts are common and perhaps inevitable in the development and maintenance of relationships, how couples manage the conflict will affect whether the conflict is constructive or destructive for the relationship. In this chapter, we will consider the role of gender in how men and women behave in a conflict situation. We will also examine the impact of gender on violence in couples' relationships.

⠶ The Demand-Withdrawal Interaction Pattern

Marcus and Christine dated one another for 3 years in college and then got married a short time after graduation. Christine works for a software computer company, and she has to travel often on sales trips. Marcus earned his degree in biotechnology, and he works at a local hospital. When Christine returns from a business trip, Marcus wants to have sex with her as a way to immediately reestablish intimacy. Christine is reluctant to have sex until she feels "close" again to Marcus. She wants to spend time together before they have sex. Marcus sulks and withdraws when Christine argues for this change in their relationship. He feels misunderstood when Christine complains that he is making "sexual demands." Also, Marcus feels uncomfortable and tense talking about his disagreements with Christine. He becomes increasingly reluctant to talk to Christine about their differences, whereas Christine feels bewildered that they are talking less and less about their problem. When Christine demands again that they talk about their difficulties, Marcus withdraws from the conversation.

A frequently observed communication pattern among couples with relationship problems is the demand/withdrawal pattern: One partner "pressures the other with demands, complaints, and criticisms, while the [other] partner withdraws with defensiveness and passive interaction" (Christensen & Shenk, 1991, p. 458). Marital satisfaction for husbands and wives is negatively associated with the degree to which couples use the demand/withdrawal pattern in a conflict situation, and wives are more likely to be the demanders and husbands to be the withdrawers (Christensen & Heavey, 1993; Noller & White, 1990). The demand/withdraw pattern of interaction can easily become a vicious cycle. As one partner presses the other to talk about a

problem and the other withdraws and avoids discussion, the first
partner feels an even greater need to talk and so may increase the
pressure to have the discussion. The increase in demand may make
the withdrawer feel even greater concern about the dangers of
discussion and an even greater need to avoid and withdraw.

Table 5.1 presents a questionnaire, developed by Christensen
and Sullaway (see Christensen, 1988; Christensen & Heavey, 1993),
that measures the extent to which the demand/withdrawal pattern is reported to occur for a heterosexual couple. There are three
items in which the woman is in the demanding role and the man
is in the withdrawing role. There are also three items in which the
roles are reversed so that the man is in the demanding role and the
woman is in the withdrawing role. The woman demand/man
withdraw interaction is represented by the sum of the scores on
the first three items. The man demand/woman withdraw interaction is represented by the sum of the last three items.

Women might demand and men might withdraw in conflict
situations because women in distressed relationships want more
change generally from their partner. However, whoever is more
invested in a particular change in the relationship (either the
woman or the man) might be expected to take on the demanding
role and the other partner the withdrawing role. Heavey, Layne,
and Christensen (1993) tested the idea that a wife demand/hus-
band withdrawal pattern was more likely when discussing an
issue considered important by the wife, whereas a husband
demand/wife withdrawal pattern was more likely when discussing an issue considered important by the husband.

Married couples were asked to talk for 7 minutes each about a
topic in which the husband wanted change in the wife's behavior
(husband's issue) and a topic in which the wife wanted a change
in the husband's behavior (wife's issue). Before the actual
problem-solving discussion, the husband and wife filled out a
self-report questionnaire about what would typically happen if
they discussed the husband's issue and the wife's issue (using the
demand/withdrawal questionnaire items in Table 5.1). Observers
also watched videotapes of the couples' discussions and provided
ratings on the wife demand/husband withdrawal and the hus-

Table 5.1 Self-Report Measure of Demand/Withdraw Interaction

	Very Unlikely								Very Likely
Woman Demands/Man Withdraws									
When some problem in the relationship arises, Woman tries to start a discussion while Man tries to avoid discussion	1	2	3	4	5	6	7	8	9
During a discussion of a relationship problem:									
Woman nags and demands while Man withdraws, becomes silent, or refuses to discuss the matter further	1	2	3	4	5	6	7	8	9
Woman criticizes while Man defends himself	1	2	3	4	5	6	7	8	9
Man Demands/Woman Withdraws									
When some problem in the relationship arises, Man tries to start a discussion while Woman tries to avoid a discussion	1	2	3	4	5	6	7	8	9
During a discussion of a relationship problem:									
Man nags and demands while Woman withdraws, becomes silent, or refuses to discuss the matter further	1	2	3	4	5	6	7	8	9
Man criticizes while Woman defends herself	1	2	3	4	5	6	7	8	9

SOURCE: From Christensen and Heavey (1993), p. 116. Used by permission of Andrew Christensen, Christopher L. Heavey, and Sage Publications.

band demand/wife withdrawal patterns. Figure 5.1 summarizes the results for demand/withdrawal based on the couples' reports and the observers' ratings. During the discussion of the wife's issue, the wife demand/husband withdrawal pattern was more likely than the husband demand/wife withdrawal pattern. During the discussion of the husband's issue, there was no difference in wife demand/husband withdrawal versus husband demand/wife withdrawal. Thus, women were more demanding and men were more withdrawing about issues where the woman desired a change in the relationship. During the discussion of an issue where the husband desired a change in the relationship, there was no clear gender-linked division in demand/withdrawal roles.

These findings suggest that couples distinguish between the woman's and the man's issue in a relationship and may be more willing, as a couple, to engage in discussion of the man's issue. Whose issue it is also affects the impact of demand/withdrawal on relationship satisfaction.

Heavey, Christensen, and Malamuth (1995) asked heterosexual couples to spend 10 minutes talking about and trying to resolve each of two issues which the man and the woman, respectively, said were a source of dissatisfaction in the relationship. Observers were trained to rate videotapes of these interactions based on ratings on a Demand scale (e.g., blames, accuses, criticizes as well as requests, demands, nags, and pressures the partner to change) and a Withdrawal scale (e.g., withdraws and avoids discussing the topic). Demand/withdrawal scales were created by summing the demand score of one partner with the withdrawal score of the other partner. Couples also completed a relationship satisfaction measure when they participated in the videotaping of their problem-solving interactions. About 2 1/2 years after the videotapes of the discussions were made, the couples were asked to provide a follow-up measure of relationship satisfaction.

Results indicated that the more the man withdrew from the interaction (i.e., he avoided discussing the topic) during the discussions of a woman's issue, the greater the decline in the women's satisfaction with the relationship over the 2 1/2-year

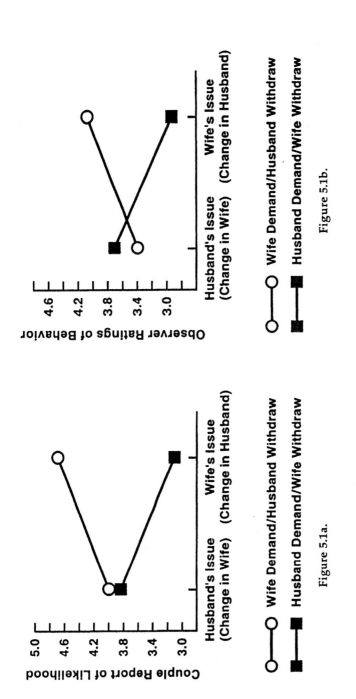

Figure 5.1a. Couple Reports of Demand/Withdraw Interaction
Figure 5.1b. Observer Ratings of Demand/Withdraw Interaction

SOURCE: From Heavey, Layne, & Christensen (1993), p. 21. Used by permission of Christopher L. Heavey, Christopher Layne, Andrew Christensen, and the American Psychological Association.

time period. Also, the more the woman demand/man withdrawal pattern occurred during the problem-solving interactions, the more the women's relationship satisfaction declined. There was a trend for men's satisfaction to be negatively correlated with man withdraws and woman demands/man withdraws measures on the woman's issues, but these results were not significant. The man withdrawal measure on discussions of men's issues was also associated with a decline in men's relationship satisfaction. Interestingly, man demands and man demands/woman withdraws during discussions of issues raised by a woman were related to an increase in women's satisfaction.

Heavey et al.'s (1995) results suggest that couples in which a man withdraws when a woman demands changes about a problem or issue she brings up are especially likely to have long-term problems. Also, the finding that the man demands pattern predicted a long-term increase in relationship satisfaction for women is intriguing (also see Heavey et al., 1993, who found that observer ratings of husband demand/wife withdraw pattern predicted long-term relationship satisfaction for wives). Perhaps a husband who actively participates in the problem-solving discussion (even if he behaves negatively, in the sense of blaming and pressuring her to change) may be showing a commitment to resolving problems that predicts long-term satisfaction. Unfortunately, the man demand/woman withdraw pattern also occurs among couples where the husband is physically abusive, suggesting that this pattern may be associated with violent power struggles and tensions (see Babcock, Waltz, Jacobson, & Gottman, 1993).

Research and reports of family therapists suggest that the woman demand/man withdraw interaction is more frequent than the man demand/woman withdraw interaction, especially when unhappy couples discuss their problems (Christensen & Heavey, 1993). Why does this woman demand/man withdraw pattern occur? One explanation focuses on the notion that men traditionally retain power or privileges by "keeping things as they are" in a relationship with their female partner (e.g., husbands are likely to do less housework, spend less time in child care). Men might have less desire to restructure or change the relationship; hence, they might want to avoid or show no interest in discussing a topic that involves a change in the status quo with their female partner. As Peplau and Gordon (1985) note,

> If men have greater power in a relationship, they may have nothing to gain by discussing problems with their partner and may benefit from avoidance. If women have lesser power, they may see confrontation as the only way to protect or to enhance their own positions. (p. 275)

⁂ Gender Stereotypes About How Men and Women Cope With Conflict

There is a controversy in the literature on conflict about the importance of gender in how males and females cope with conflict (see Canary, Cupach, & Messman, 1995; Cupach & Canary, 1995; O'Donohue & Crouch, 1996). Partners' perceptions of gender differences in how males and females deal with conflict might be greater than behavioral differences observed in a laboratory setting, where couples are videotaped and asked to talk about a relationship problem—at least when intact and well-functioning couples are studied (Markman, Silvern, Clements, & Kraft-Hanak, 1993). Hence, couples' stereotypes about how men and women discuss relationship problems may influence their own reports of what happened, which may or may not mirror what actually occurred between them. It should be noted, however, that stereotypes or beliefs about gender differences may have an impact on a couple's relationship in terms of how partners feel and act toward one another. If, for instance, women think that men are withdrawn and avoidant, women may engage in pursuit behaviors as a response. If men think that women are critical and demanding, men may engage in withdrawal behaviors as a response. Thus, gender-linked expectancies about how someone reacts to a conflict may affect behavior toward one's partner so that these beliefs are subsequently confirmed by the other's behavior (Markman et al., 1993).

Couples and perhaps marital therapists need to be careful not to exaggerate how often the female demand and male withdrawal pattern occurs among nondistressed couples. Nevertheless, as conflicts increase for a couple, females and males may fall back on traditional gender-linked patterns of behavior.

Is There a Physiological Explanation for Why Men May Withdraw From High Conflict Situations?

Reviewing 20 years of research on marital interactions, Gottman (1994) in his book *What Predicts Divorce?* concludes that during highly stressful arguments, husbands, compared to wives, tend to withdraw from the interactions (involving a refusal to respond to the partner, called "stonewalling"), whereas wives, compared to husbands, tend to complain and criticize. Gottman videotapes couples' interactions during conflict discussions and then uses a comprehensive coding scheme to rate the husbands' and wives' behaviors. Stonewalling, according to Gottman, tends to occur in highly stressful, negatively loaded situations where both partners express a lot of negative feelings toward one another, such as defensiveness (Why are you bothering me?) and contempt (How can you be so stupid?). Gottman argues that men cannot cope as well as women in highly stressful (or negative) interpersonal situations. Men may be more susceptible to physiological arousal during high conflict discussions and, hence, they may find such situations more unpleasant. Males, according to Gottman (1994), tend to withdraw from these interactions or stonewall to escape the high level of physiological arousal. However, a paradoxical effect of this withdrawal may be to increase physiological arousal even further. The partner who is stonewalling may mentally obsess about why he is upset (e.g., My partner won't leave me alone), leading him to become even more aroused and withdrawn.

How Do Same-Sex Couples Handle Conflict?

In distressed marriages and in high conflict discussions, women are more likely than men to make demands (including complaining and criticizing). Men, on the other hand, are more likely than women to withdraw (including avoiding a discussion of the problem, becoming silent, and refusing to respond). If, as Gottman (1994) argues, women are better able than men to cope with negative emotions in their interactions, lesbians and gay men may handle conflict in their love relationships differently. The interaction of a gay male couple might be oriented to avoiding high conflict discussions by attempting to reconcile one another's disagreements before the conflict escalates. But the gay men may withdraw from a discussion of the problem if a topic of high conflict occurs. The interaction of a lesbian couple might be oriented to confronting the conflict and expressing lots of feelings (both positive and negative).

There may be a physiological explanation for why gay men, compared to lesbians, might withdraw from high conflict interactions: because men find the expression of negative feelings more unpleasant than women do (Gottman, 1994). Gay men, however, may have difficulty communicating their negative (and positive feelings) about an issue in the couple's relationship because they (like heterosexual men) may have adopted a rigid and stereotyped view of how "real men" are supposed to behave. Gay men may avoid expressing intense negative feelings in order to avoid fitting into cultural stereotypes that gay men are highly emotional and "feminine." Hence, a gay male couple may inhibit the disclosure of feelings to maintain a macho pose of being "rational" and "cool" in the face of a relationship problem (see Brown, 1995).

⁂ How Males and Females May Be Alike in Coping With Conflict: Relationship Types

There are also similarities between men and women in many couples in how they handle conflict. For instance, Gottman (1993, 1994) suggests that there are three types of "stable" couples based on how husbands and wives rely on different communication styles to deal with conflict (also see Fitzpatrick, 1987, 1988). *Conflict-avoiding* couples attempt to minimize conflict; *volatile* couples are emotionally expressive, being willing to engage in conflict and to try to change their partner's opinions; and *validating* couples try to avoid conflict, but they will argue about important matters in their relationship. Interestingly, Gottman (1993, 1994) presents evidence that the avoidant, volatile, and validating couples may all represent stable, nondistressed relationships. Whatever their coping styles in handling conflict, the three types of couples have a high proportion of pleasant to unpleasant experiences during their interactions with one another (roughly a five to one ratio of positive to negative events). On the other hand, Gottman (1993, 1994) documents that there are two types of unstable relationships where the partners both tend to be negative in their conversations with one another. There may be a lot of direct criticisms but also defensiveness on the part of the partners (so-called *hostile* couples); or partners may be emotionally uninvolved and detached, lashing out occasionally at one another in episodes of mutual criticism and defensiveness (so-called *hostile/detached* couples). This work on different types of intimate couples (based on how they cope with conflict) indicates the importance of studying possible similarities in how men and women cope with disagreements.

Physical Assaults

> It's been almost 3 years since I replaced the locks on the front door. It took months just for me to stop jumping at shadows in the courtyard. In our 14 months together, no single day was worse than the one I was caught off guard, pulled from the shower, and thrown onto our bed, dripping and naked.
>
> It had been a tequila sunrise for him. Like Mel Gibson in the movie, he slammed his open palm across first the right side of my face and then the left. Once, twice, I don't know how many times. Never one to cower, I pushed him against the window a little too hard and, for a second, thought how lovely it would be if we could just fall to the ground and die together. He had been jealous—insanely jealous—before, but this was his first real physical outburst. He accused me of lying—of not being where I said I was. He made up lies to "trick" me into some sort of confession. I had no idea what he was talking about. (Zook, 1996, p. C5)*

---

* Material used by permission. Copyright ©1996 by Kristal Brent Zook.

We might prefer to think that physical assaults occur in interactions with strangers or nonromantic partners. However, the results of surveys conducted in the United States indicate that physical assaults occur frequently in couples. For instance, Straus and Gelles (1990b) conducted a national telephone survey of more than 6,000 randomly selected U.S. households in the summer of 1985. They found "that just over 16% or one out of six American couples experienced an incident involving a physical assault during 1985" (Straus & Gelles, 1990b, p. 96). In roughly half these couples, both partners had been violent; in about one quarter of the cases, the husband was violent but the wife was not violent; and in the other quarter, the wife was violent but the husband was not violent.

The term "the marriage license as a hitting license" (Stets & Straus, 1990b, p. 227) has been coined to reflect the high assault rate that occurs in married couples in comparison to the assault rate that occurs between strangers. But studies indicate that dating or cohabiting couples have a higher rate of physical assault than married couples. For instance, Stets and Straus (1990b) used data from the 1985 Family Violence Survey (see Straus & Gelles, 1990b) and from a sample of students at a midwestern American university. About 35% of the cohabiting couples and 20% of the dating couples reported at least one physical assault occurring during the previous year, whereas about 15% of the married couples reported a physical assault during the previous year. Using a representative sample of college women and men, White and Koss (1991) also found a high rate of physical aggression among dating couples. White and Koss (1991) found that "about 37% of the men and 35% of the women [in their national sample] inflicted some form of physical aggression, and about 39% of the men and 32% of the women sustained some physical aggression" (p. 247).

Although the incidence of physical violence may be high in "bad" or "stressful" relationships (see Marshall, 1994, pp. 290-291), violence also occurs among couples who report satisfaction with their relationship. For instance, one study that sought to recruit "satisfied" couples for research on marital violence found that 23.5% of the husbands had physically abused their spouses at some point in their relationship and 12% had physically abused their partner in the preceding year (Holtzworth-Munroe et al.,

1992). Thus violence may occur in relationships that are bad, but it may also occur in relationships that are supposedly nondistressed or "normal."

Violence is commonly defined as "an act carried out with the intention or perceived intention of causing physical pain or injury to another person" (see Feld & Straus, 1990, p. 490). However, it should be noted that the aggressor may or may not intend to harm the victim; the aggressive action may be instrumental in getting one's way without the intent to cause injury per se. Also, although the aggressor may be angry and want to hurt the victim, the physical assault may or may not be related to an immediate conflict. For instance, battered women sometimes report that they were "hit 'out of the clear blue sky' without a prior or concurrent conflictual interaction" (Marshall, 1994, p. 283). Finally, although violent acts may be intended to cause injury, they may also occur in the context of attempting to defend oneself or to stop the other's physical assault.

⁂ Gender Differences in Physical Aggressiveness

There is controversy about whether or not men and women are similar or different in how violent they are in their intimate relationships (Koss et al., 1994). The debate is based mainly on how to interpret partners' responses to the Conflict Tactics Scale developed by Straus (1990). This scale provides ratings of three ways of dealing with conflict: (1) reasoning (e.g., Discussed an issue calmly; Brought in, or tried to bring in, someone to help settle things); (2) verbal aggression (e.g., Did or said something to spite him/her; Threatened to hit or throw something at him/her); and (3) physical aggression or violence (e.g., Threw something at him/her; Pushed, grabbed, or shoved him/her; Slapped him/her; Beat him/her; Threatened him/her with a knife or gun).

Based on responses to the Conflict Tactics Scale (see Table 5.2), Straus and Gelles (1990a) reported that "the rates for violence by wives are remarkably similar to the rates for violence by husbands" (p. 96). This research documented that about 11.6% of husbands reported that they had carried out at least one act of violence against their spouse during the last year (e.g., slapping, pushing, hitting, threatening with or using a knife or gun), whereas 12.4% of the wives reported that they had carried out at least one act of violence against their spouse during the last year. We noted earlier a study by White and Koss (1991) which also found that females and males (college students in dating relationships) were approximately equal in their reports of inflicting or sustaining some type of physical aggression (e.g., hitting, grabbing, or shoving). White and Koss's (1991) data were based on participants' self-reports on the Conflict Tactics Scale (Straus, 1990).

It would be inappropriate to conclude from these results with the Conflict Tactics Scale that women are "about as violent as men" (Straus & Gelles, 1990a, p. 104) in their intimate relationships. This research does not take account of the motivations for the physical aggressiveness, whether the violence is intended to injure the partner, or whether it is intended for self-defense or retaliation. The research using the Conflict Tactics Scale also tends to blur distinctions about similarities and differences in physical aggression among males and females because only a relatively few types of aggressive acts are measured. For example, the research suggesting that physical violence may be equal for both women and men does not take into account that men more than women use sexual assault as a form of aggression (Koss et al., 1994; Marshall, 1994).

Women, compared to men, also suffer greater physical and emotional harm from these violent episodes. Consider the results of a study examining the impact of physical aggression among unhappily married couples seeking psychological treatment (Cascardi, Langhinrichsen, & Vivian, 1992). About 71% of the couples reported at least one act of physical aggression during the previous year. Pushing, grabbing, and shoving were the most frequently reported "mildly" aggressive acts, whereas kicking, biting, and hitting with a fist were the most frequently reported "severely" aggressive acts. Women were more likely than men to sustain a severe physical injury from these violent acts. About 15% of the wives who were involved in a mildly aggressive incident and 11% of the wives who were involved in a severely

Table 5.2 Measuring the Use of Verbal and Physical Aggression

The statements for the Conflict Tactics Scale are presented below. Items a through c emphasize the use of verbal reasoning, items d through j emphasize verbal/symbolic aggression, and items k through s emphasize the use of physical force or violence to solve a conflict. Item g, "cried," is not included on any subscale although it is included in the questionnaire. Ask yourself how often (if ever) you and your relationship partner did the things described in the statements in the past year when you had a dispute or disagreement.

	Never	One Time	More Than Once
a. Discussed the issue calmly	1	2	3
b. Got information to back up (your/[partner's]) side of things	1	2	3
c. Brought in or tried to bring in someone to help settle things	1	2	3
d. Insulted or swore at the other one	1	2	3
e. Sulked and/or refused to talk about it	1	2	3
f. Stomped out of the room or house (or yard)	1	2	3
g. Cried	1	2	3
h. Did or said something to spite the other one	1	2	3
i. Threatened to hit or throw something at the other one	1	2	3
j. Threw or smashed or hit or kicked something	1	2	3
k. Threw something at the other one	1	2	3
l. Pushed, grabbed, or shoved the other one	1	2	3
m. Slapped the other one	1	2	3
n. Kicked, bit, or hit with a fist	1	2	3
o. Hit or tried to hit with something	1	2	3
p. Beat up the other one	1	2	3
q. Choked the other one	1	2	3
r. Threatened with a knife or gun	1	2	3
s. Used a knife or gun	1	2	3

If a large number of individuals completed the form (e.g., among students in a class), you could find out the overall percentage of individuals who report *never, once,* or *more than once* "inflicting" and "sustaining" various forms of verbal/symbolic and physical aggression, as well as the percentage of individuals using different types of verbal reasoning to cope with conflicts. You could also examine whether there are gender differences in inflicting and sustaining the various types of verbal/symbolic and physical aggression. Also, you might want to discuss with the class how frequently various actions were used during a particular incident.

SOURCE: From Straus (1990), p. 33. Used by permission of Murray A. Straus.

aggressive incident suffered broken bones, broken teeth, or damage to sensory organs. On the other hand, just 2% of the husbands who were involved in a mildly aggressive incident and none of the husbands who were involved in a severely aggressive incident suffered broken bones, broken teeth, or damage to sensory organs. The wives, compared to the husbands, also rated the psychological impact of mild and/or severe physical aggression as more negative. The results of Cascardi et al.'s (1992) study are consistent with other research indicating that, although men and women may both be likely to engage in and experience physical aggression in their intimate relationships, women are at greater risk than men of being severely injured physically and of suffering negative emotional consequences from their spouse's aggression (see Koss et al., 1994; Stets & Straus, 1990a).

The debate over the relative frequency of male versus female reciprocal violence in intimate relationships, and a reexamination of the data and their sources led Johnson (1995) to propose that there are two distinct forms of violence: patriarchal terrorism and common couple violence. He argues that the gender equality found in national surveys of domestic violence reflects common couple violence, the fighting that occurs in couples when arguments "get out of hand." This violence is sporadic, it rarely escalates, it may be initiated by women or men, and it seldom leads to serious injury. On the other hand,

> Patriarchal terrorism, a product of patriarchal traditions of men's right to control "their" women, is a form of terroristic control of wives by their husbands that involves the systematic use of not only violence, but economic subordination, threats, isolation, and other control tactics. (Johnson, 1995, p. 284)

Women seen in shelters are more likely to be experiencing patriarchal terrorism than common couple violence. Thus, the debate between researchers collecting data from shelters and emergency rooms where the population is almost entirely women and researchers reporting on data from large surveys that find equal numbers of women and men reporting violent behavior may result from their observing qualitatively (and often quantitatively) different types of violence.

✒ Interaction Patterns in Couples
With a Violent Husband

There has been considerable interest recently in understanding the dynamics of physically abusive husbands and their wives—given concerns about domestic violence and risks of injury (particularly to wives and children when husbands are violent). One major explanation for male violence is that husbands (and men generally) were traditionally expected to control and even physically "chastise" their wives. Thus, a patriarchal power structure that supports and maintains males' beliefs in their superiority over women might tolerate and even excuse wife beating. Most men, even in a patriarchal culture, do not beat their partners. Nevertheless, if men imagine or perceive a challenge or threat to their power, control, or authority, they may use physical violence to reassert their authority (Baumeister, Smart, & Boden, 1996; Yllo & Straus, 1990). This is the form of couples violence that Johnson (1995) has labeled patriarchal terrorism.

One way that men might perceive their power in a relationship as threatened would be if males felt they were deficient in communication skills (e.g., being unable to express ideas in a clear and orderly manner). Thus, men who are unskilled as communicators may use physical violence because they perceive that there is no other way to handle a conflict or dispute with their partner. Also, if men feel threatened in their decision-making power (i.e., if men do not believe they have "the final say" in making decisions), they may be more likely to be violent, especially as an extreme way of reasserting control.

A recent study by Babcock et al. (1993) provides evidence that husbands' poor communication skills and their perception of lacking decision-making power are associated with the use of physical violence by men in handling marital conflicts. We focus on data reported in the article about husbands who had any history of being physically aggressive toward their wives. The authors found that husbands who had lower communication skills (based on judges' ratings of the husbands' ability to express their ideas during an interview) were more likely to have used physical violence during previous marital disputes. Husbands who perceived that they had less power than their wives in making decisions (e.g., about household tasks, raising children) were more likely to have used physical violence in the past during marital disputes. The wives' poor communication skills were positively associated with the amount of physical violence displayed by the husband during conflicts. Thus, at least among husbands who show a propensity for physical violence, husbands' violence is likely to increase if the husband *and* the wife have poor communication skills and if the husband perceives that he has relatively low decision-making power.

Readers may recall that among distressed marital couples and in high conflict situations, women are more likely to be in the demand role whereas men are more likely to be in the withdraw role. It has been suggested that the demand role for women might be associated with a position of low power in a relationship. The partner who presses the spouse to discuss a problem and then criticizes, nags, and makes demands may perceive herself to be in a less powerful position than the person who wants to keep the status quo. Babcock et al. (1993) found *in domestically violent married couples* that husbands who reported increased husband demand/wife withdrawal in handling conflict situations were more likely to use physical aggression in the marital relationship. Interestingly, when these couples were compared to couples that had no history of domestic violence but were dissatisfied with their marriages (maritally distressed/nonviolent couples) and to couples that had no history of domestic violence and were satisfied with their marriages (maritally happy/nonviolent couples), Babcock et al. (1993) found the husband demand/wife withdraw interaction pattern was more likely among domestically violent than among the distressed/nonviolent or happy/nonviolent couples. The wife demand/husband withdraw interaction pattern was more likely among domestically violent and distressed/nonviolent couples than among happy/nonviolent couples. As Babcock et al. (1993) conclude, "wife demand/husband withdraw may have more to do with marital distress than with domestic violence" (p. 47). In contrast, husband demand/wife withdraw may be more uniquely associated with domestic violence— husbands may rely on physical aggression to make up for a perceived absence of power to cope with conflict in their relationships.

The study conducted by Babcock et al. (1993) suggests how some men may use physical aggression to counteract a sense of being less powerful than the woman in an intimate relationship. It would be worthwhile, however, to examine directly how physically abusive husbands and their wives deal with conflict situations. For instance, if husbands' physical aggressiveness is designed to control, it might be expected that wives, in comparison to husbands, would report being afraid during arguments. The fear that the husband might be violent could be an effective technique to control the wife's behavior. Also, if physical aggression by the husband is a form of control, it might be relatively difficult for wives to predict when male violence will occur. If females cannot predict when the male's violence will occur, they may experience his behavior as less controllable. A recently conducted study by Jacobson et al. (1994) provides answers to these questions.

Two groups of married couples were studied. One group was formed from couples that had experienced a high level of male-to-female violence in the last year (the domestic violence group). In this group, according to the wives,

> 36% had been beaten up within the past year; 75% had been kicked, bitten, or hit; 21% of the husbands had been arrested on a domestic violence charge; and 80% of the wives had been injured by their husbands' actions, 23% seriously enough to seek medical attention. (Jacobson et al., 1994, p. 983)

A second group of maritally distressed but nonviolent couples also participated in the study. Couples were interviewed in a laboratory situation concerning how they interacted during arguments at home. Also, couples talked in the laboratory about two areas where they had continuing disagreements between them.

During the discussions of disagreements in the laboratory, both husbands and wives in the domestic violence group expressed more anger compared to the husbands and wives in the distressed/nonviolent group. Consistent with the idea that men may use fear of violence as a method of controlling their wives' behavior, women in the domestic violence group displayed more tension or fear than women in the nonviolent group during the interaction, even though men in the domestic violence group did not display more violence than men in the nonviolent group. As Jacobson et al. (1994) note, "only husband violence produces fear in the partner" (p. 986).

The researchers examined whether there was anything that wives could do in abusive relationships to predict or control their husbands' violent behavior. The reports of wives indicated that husbands would continue their violence when the wife was violent herself, when she tried to verbally defend herself, or when she attempted to withdraw from the interaction. The husbands tended to agree with their wives' reports, reporting that their violence would continue when the wife was violent or if she was being verbally aggressive. Both the wives' and the husbands' reports indicated that there was nothing the wife could do to suppress the husband's violent behavior once it had begun. Thus, women had little control over their husband's violence. Whether the wife tried to withdraw from the interaction or to fight back, neither action was likely to stop the husband from being violent. Based on these results, if women cannot stop male violence once it begins, they may experience a sense of powerlessness in the relationship.

⁊⯑ Violence in Same-Sex Couples

Jim and Michael have been living together in a committed romantic relationship for the past year. The two men describe their feelings for each other as "love at first sight." After dating for only a month, the two move in together. At first, the relationship seems perfect—loving, supportive, and sexually satisfying. However, after about 6 months, Michael starts to belittle Jim, first criticizing his style of dress, then his accent, friends, and housecleaning habits. Michael also begins to badger Jim if he comes home late from work about where he's been and with whom. One night, Michael escalates his inquisition and starts accusing Jim of seeing other men. Jim denies the accusations but becomes angry and shouts at Michael to leave him alone. Michael becomes enraged, punches Jim in the face, and knocks him down. Michael apologizes and promises he will never do that again. Jim is upset, but he accepts Michael's apology. Three weeks later, Michael breaks his promise. This time he cracks one of Jim's ribs.

Two lesbians, Maria and Pat, started dating about 8 months ago. They are very strongly attracted to each other and soon start spending all their free time together. The couple almost always spends their time at Pat's house because Pat's cats require daily care. About a month ago, Maria began to feel dissatisfied with this arrangement. She misses her old friends and her apartment. She tells Pat she is very committed to her but wants to do more things separately. Pat is very upset. She begins to argue with Maria any time Maria makes plans to see anyone else or wants to go to her apartment. She accuses Maria of being unable to make a commitment to a relationship and questions whether Maria is really a lesbian. Then, Maria tells Pat she wants to break up. Pat begins stalking Maria, leaving notes on her car at work and calling her at all hours during the night. One night, Maria is walking home from a nearby restaurant and Pat comes up beside her and grabs her arm. She tells Maria, "I'll never let you go." When Maria tries to pull away, Pat begins hitting her.

The literature on violence in intimate relationships has mainly focused on heterosexual couples who are either married, dating, or living together. But physical abuse also occurs in some same-sex relationships (Island & Letellier, 1991; Renzetti, 1992). We do not know as much about violence in gay male or lesbian couples, in part, because of the "invisibility" often associated with same-sex couples (Brown, 1995). For instance, gay couples may keep a low profile about their relationships to avoid being criticized or rejected by heterosexual friends, family members, or coworkers. Nevertheless, same-sex couples, just like "straight" couples, experience difficulties in their relationships. These problems (whether interpersonal—e.g., overdependence, excessive jealousy; or intrapersonal—e.g., overreliance on alcohol, inability to cope with stress at work), in turn, can contribute to partners hitting or physically hurting one another. All partners (same-sex and heterosexual) must acknowledge that physical violence is never acceptable or normal regardless of the degree of the couples' disagreements; violence is the responsibility of the person who is being abusive in the relationship, not the victim; partners must find nonviolent ways to express their anger without hitting their partner.

Conclusions

We have examined the role of gender in affecting how couples deal with conflict and violence in their relationships. Males, compared to females, are more likely to withdraw from conflict, particularly in unhappy relationships and in highly stressful discussions. Although research findings are still preliminary, men's withdrawal in the face of conflict may be due either to men's resistance to changing the status quo in a current situation or to men's discomfort with expressing intensely negative emotions. Women, on the other hand, may be more expressive of their negative feelings about a relationship issue because they are more dissatisfied with the status quo or they may be simply more comfortable expressing negative feelings. Unfortunately, in many physically abusive relationships, one or both partners—females and males—may *have* highly negative feelings about their partner that may spill over into physical aggressiveness. Couples must learn that violence in a relationship does not "just happen" and that beating or hitting one's partner is *never* acceptable.

This chapter has focused on gender differences in conflict and violence. However, it should be noted that couples are unique and any two individuals (female-male, female-female, or male-male) will develop their distinctive ways of dealing with problems (or even the threat of violence) in their relationship. The ultimate value of studying the impact of gender on conflict and violence may rest in the light it sheds on how other factors affect coping with conflict (e.g., balance of power in relationships, ease or difficulty in expressing negative feelings, and the role of patriarchal societal structures, which traditionally gave the male partner authority and advantage over the female partner).

6

Friendship

The bird a nest, the spider a web, man friendship.
William Blake (1757-1827)

It's the friends that you can call up at 4 a.m. that matter.
Marlene Dietrich (b. 1904)

Most women and men are well aware of the importance of friendship in their lives, but psychologists only recently have begun to study friendship and how it is affected by gender (O'Connor, 1992; Winstead, 1986). In Western culture, friendship is defined by the values reserved for close personal relationships, including affection, trust, and loyalty. Within the United States specifically, expressive intimacy is viewed as a particularly important aspect of close relationships such as friendship (e.g., Bank,

1994; Cancian, 1987). Thus, as expressed in the two quotations above, a friend is someone who may be called in the middle of the night to provide comfort and support. In addition, friendship is a voluntary relationship; it is not shaped by laws or regulations. Consequently, a friendship has no formal ending. Instead, disappointments or conflicts sometimes cause friends to break up or drift apart.

Six specific rules that have been shown to contribute to maintaining same-sex friendships include standing up for the friend in her/his absence; sharing news of success with the friend; showing emotional support; trusting and confiding in each other; volunteering help in time of need; and striving to make the friend happy while in each other's company (Argyle & Henderson, 1984). Beyond these rules, certain aspects of same-sex friendship differ for women and men. Women's friendships tend to be more intimate than men's, whereas men's are more activity-oriented, according to some research (e.g., Duck & Wright, 1993). Cross-sex friendships also appear to operate somewhat differently from same-sex friendships, at least among heterosexuals. For instance, they are more difficult to establish and pose other challenges that must be negotiated, such as sexual attraction (e.g., O'Meara, 1994).

The preceding examples illustrate that discussions of friendship in a broad sense quickly must be qualified by references to gender and, to some extent, sexual orientation. This does not mean that women's and men's friendships are always different or that one kind of friendship is superior to another. Rather, it illustrates that the same general processes concerning gender and romantic interactions also affect friendship.

≈ Gender Roles and Relationships

Gender differences in friendships have been linked to patterns of gender socialization. Typically, girls are socialized to be interdependent, cooperative, and emotionally attuned to others, whereas boys are taught to be independent, competitive, and dominant (Maccoby, 1990; Maltz & Borker, 1983). As a result, girls and boys develop different values concerning what is important in friendship and learn to interact according to the norms of their same-sex group. Maccoby has described norms for girls as emphasizing an *enabling style* of interaction, whereas norms for boys encourage a *restrictive style*. An enabling style is one that supports whatever the partner is doing and tends to keep the interaction going. Agreeing with the partner, acknowledging another's comment, and taking turns talking are examples. An enabling style appears to be conducive to establishing intimate relationships such as friendship and may be related to a preference among girls and women for private dyadic or small-group interactions. In contrast, a restrictive style tends to derail the interaction, either shortening or ending it. Examples are boasting, contradicting, interrupting, or threatening a partner. A restrictive style is well suited to large, hierarchically organized group activities such as team sports.

Gender socialization and gender segregation are two processes that are believed to contribute jointly to the development of gender norms (Thorne, 1986). Gender socialization by adults reinforces the expression of different emotions and play interests in girls and boys (Unger & Crawford, 1996). For example, teachers and parents, particularly fathers, more frequently reward help-seeking behavior in girls and emphasize sadness as an emotion rather than anger. Adults also are more likely to select environments for girls that include delicate and restrictive clothing and toys such as dolls and kitchen items. In contrast, boys are encouraged to develop athletic skills, to roam farther from adults, and to engage in rough play. Durable clothing more often is selected for boys, as are toy vehicles and sports equipment. These socialization practices help to shape children's feelings, activities, and interests along gender-typed lines.

Gender segregation is a second important process related to gender differences and has a strong impact on friendships. Social interaction among children is strongly separated by gender. Barrie Thorne (1986) described the daily process of gender segregation occurring from preschool through fifth grade in one elementary school she observed. Although adults usually did not formally divide physical space and curricula by gender, they frequently used it as a visible marker, for example, "The girls are ready and the boys aren't." Gender also was sometimes used as a basis for organizing activities. For instance, aides defined the space close to the building as girls' territory and the playing fields (an area 10 times larger than the girls) as boys' territory. These practices make gender salient to children when friends or play activities are chosen. It also requires that play activities and interaction styles be adapted to the space and toys made available for each gender.

A considerable amount of research has documented gender differences among girls' and boys' peer groups and friendships (e.g., McCloskey & Coleman, 1992). However, there are two reasons these findings should be interpreted carefully. First, the research has not established the cause(s) of gender differences. Do girls and boys simply prefer a certain interactive style and subsequently gravitate toward situations where the style is effective, as might be suggested by individual or biological theories? For example, do boys "naturally" prefer competitive, large-group activities and girls small-group or dyadic interactions that subsequently cause boys to gravitate toward team sports and girls toward less hierarchical small-group play? Or does the structure of gender-typed activities dictate a certain interactive style that must be mastered if one wishes to participate, as suggested by structural or learning theories? That is, does sex-typed play teach boys and girls whether to prefer GI Joe or Barbie dolls, as well as to seek the approval of their same-sex peer group? These questions probably are not answerable because the social contexts of girls' and boys' worlds differ in systematic ways, as described above, making the direction of causation difficult to establish.

Second, gender differences often are overstated (Thorne, 1986). Gender differences are not necessarily permanent or dichotomous; they may vary by situation, race, social class, or culture. Considerable individual variation also exists. For example, many girls are tomboys or athletes and not all boys fight. Nor is gender segregation absolute; girls and boys sometimes play together. Thus, once individual variation and other factors are taken into account, the similarities between the sexes may far outweigh the differences.

⁂ Child and Adolescent Friendships

Children develop notions of friendship quite young, and their ideas become more abstract with age (see review by Fehr, 1996). In response to the question of what is a friend, preschool-age children identify three themes: someone who plays with you (play), someone who shares toys with you (prosocial), and someone who doesn't hit you (nonaggressive). By Grades 2 to 6, children describe friends as having five features: support (e.g., sharing or helping), spending time together, intimacy, similarity (e.g., common activities), and affection (Furman & Bierman, 1984). During adolescence, the interpersonal features of the friendship become more important, particularly *loyalty* (sticking up for each other even when the friend isn't present) and *intimacy*, defined as sharing one's innermost thoughts and feelings (e.g., Bigelow & LaGaipa, 1980). The interpersonal aspects of friendship remain significant throughout adulthood (Fehr, 1996).

Although gender differences in friendship expectations and behavior do not start to surface consistently until adolescence, a preference for same-sex friends begins as early as preschool (Maccoby & Jacklin, 1987). As noted earlier, it is not possible to determine whether children "naturally" prefer same-sex friends or the extent to which this choice is contingent on situational variables such as group size, activities, adult behavior, collective meanings, or the risk of being teased by peers or adults (Thorne, 1986).

Two factors affect same-sex friendship choice in the preschool years (Maccoby, 1988). First, interactions between boys tend to be more competitive, to include more vying for dominance, and to involve more rough play. Many girls may find this style of play to be aversive. Second, most boys are not responsive to girls' attempts to influence them. Boys' tendency to ignore girls has been observed as early as 33 months of age. As a result, interactions with boys may be unrewarding for girls, who may choose to avoid pursuing boys as friends. Boys also avoid interactions with girls even more strongly. Thus, what may begin in early childhood as a slight preference for same-sex friends may evolve into stronger preferences through the process of gender segregation and the development of peer-group norms.

Gender differences in friendship begin to emerge consistently around middle childhood, corresponding with a large increase in preference for same-sex friends occurring by age 7 (Maccoby & Jacklin, 1987). Gender-typed play preferences also increase around age 9 and appear to further reinforce same-sex friendship choice. For example, Moller, Hymel, and Rubin (1992) observed second and fourth graders in free-play sessions and found only one gender difference among second graders: Boys tended to engage in significantly more functional/sensorimotor play than girls. Among fourth graders, many differences were reported, with boys engaging in more functional/sensorimotor play, aggressive play, and group games-with-rules, and with girls engaging in more parallel (playing side-by-side but not together) and constructive play (Lego blocks, markers and paper). In addition, boys' popularity by Grade 4 was found to be significantly related to their involvement in male-preferred play. Other research suggests that gender-typed play preferences become increasingly salient with age in determining children's social reputations. Physically active boys and "nice" girls are likely to be the most popular (e.g., Hartup, 1996).

The most frequent finding concerning gender differences is that girls expect more intimacy and self-disclosure from their best friends than boys, beginning as early as second grade, but particularly by late adolescence (Fehr, 1996). Otherwise, to a large extent, girls and boys generally expect and receive similar things in friendship. Clark and Ayers (1993) investigated how much actual best same-sex friends lived up to seventh and eighth graders' expectations. Both girls and boys expected more honesty and straightforwardness from their friends than actually was received. Conversely, best friends engaged in more mutual activities with both girls and boys and were more loyal and committed to the friendship than had been expected. However, gender differences were found for empathic understanding: Girls both expected and received more empathic understanding from their best friends than boys did. This example illustrates that girls and boys are more similar than different in terms of what they expect and receive from friends, but that when differences are observed, they tend to be in the area of intimacy.

A second gender difference that has been found in some research pertains to how girls and boys respond to conflict in friendship. Although the most typical response to conflict for both sexes is the "ostrich approach" (e.g., burying one's head in the sand), when children choose other strategies, boys are more likely to be overt or direct in their response than girls (Thorne & Luria, 1986). One explanation for this difference is that girls may fear they will lose the friendship if they express anger overtly. Girls in Grades 2, 6, and 10 were more concerned than boys with avoiding conflict in friendship (Tannen, 1990). Another explanation is that aggression is more normative in boys' friendships than girls'; thus, direct expressions of anger are not necessarily perceived as a threat to the friendship. For instance, Bank (1994) reported that 10th-grade boys more often than girls identified behaviors labeled as *assertive friendship*, such as teasing, quarreling, bossiness, and competition, as being typical positive expressions of same-sex friendship.

Less is known about cross-sex friendships in childhood both because they are less frequent and less often studied (Thorne, 1986). Although relaxed cross-sex interactions sometimes occur in schools or neighborhoods, contact may not be sufficient to build a close friendship. Most cross-sex interactions are based upon and reinforce gender boundaries. Specific types of activities that maintain the *gender border* include contests that pit girls and boys against each other, rituals that label one sex as "contaminating" (e.g., girls have cooties), chasing (e.g., girls chase the boys) and invasions (e.g., boys disrupt girls' play). Heterosexual teasing (e.g., Johnny likes Karen) also frequently is aimed at children who initiate cross-sex interactions, particularly boys. As a result, cross-sex friendships are less likely to develop. Furthermore, if they do occur, they are likely to be concealed from others to avoid ridicule (Thorne, 1986).

During adolescence, cross-sex friendships are more accepted; in fact, having them increases girls' and boys' social status with same-sex peers (e.g., Epstein, 1986). Adolescents expect less from their cross-sex than same-sex friends. Cross-sex friends are chosen primarily on the basis of how sociable they are, whereas same-sex friends are expected to be intellectual peers as well as sociable.

Cross-sex friendships also tend to be less intimate (e.g., Eshel & Kurman, 1990).

In general, child and adolescent friendships provide a training ground for the development of skills that continue to be important for establishing peer and intimate relations in adulthood (Duck, 1991). Friendship also helps adolescents to forge an identity that will lead to adult autonomy (Douvan, 1983). Finally, adolescent friendships coincide with the developmental phase when fundamental decisions and life issues are being confronted for the first time. As a result, they appear to set the standard for what is meant by "real friendship" throughout life (Weiss & Lowenthal, 1975). What is important to note in terms of gender is that these standards are usually situated within the context of same-sex friendship.

ꙮ Adult Same-Sex Friendships

Danielle and Kara have been close friends since high school. Although they go to different colleges, they keep in touch by sending audiocassette "letters" to each other. They renew their friendship in person during their summer breaks at home. What they like most about the friendship is having fun together; they enjoy just talking about their lives and goals, swimming, playing softball, double dating, shopping, and pursuing their interest in Native American artifacts and crafts.

Jamal and Steve consider each other to be best friends. They met in the dorm 2 years ago and discovered they had a mutual enthusiasm for alternative music. They spend a lot of their time listening to new artists and swapping music trivia. On Thursday nights, they usually play basketball with a bunch of guys from the dorm. Jamal teases Steve a lot about his taste in women; in turn, Steve jokes about Jamal's high standards for women, friends, and cars. They are planning to room together next year.

These two friendship profiles illustrate some of the typical functions of friendship in young adulthood. Intimacy, help, companionship, and acceptance most often are mentioned as important functions of same-sex friendships by young adults (Rose, 1985). Friendships also provide a social support system that enables young adults to separate from family and reduces the feelings of loneliness that tend to be stronger at this stage of life than others (Rawlins, 1992).

Interestingly, the above profiles could be used to illustrate both gender differences and gender similarities in friendship. For instance, some evidence has shown that women's friendships are more expressive (focusing on the socioemotional aspects of the relationship), and men's are more instrumental (emphasizing the tasks and goals associated with the friendship over the intimate aspects) (e.g., Wright & Scanlon, 1991). Women's friendships also have been reported as being affectively richer, involving more self-disclosure, and as more communal than men's (e.g., Brehm, 1992). The face-to-face and "all-purpose" qualities of women's friendship have been contrasted by Wright (1988) with the "side-by-side" activity focus of men's friendships. Similarly, Danielle and Kara's friendship could be described as dyadic or face-to-face, as well as highly intimate and self-disclosing. It is also all-purpose, with the friends engaging in a range of activities with each other. Conversely, Jamal and Steve's friendship could be described as being side-by-side, with interactions primarily focusing on specific tasks and activities and also including more group activities. Their good-natured but mildly aggressive teasing and low level of direct self-disclosure fits the stereotypic pattern for male peer groups.

Other evidence points to the existence of considerable gender similarities in friendship. Duck and Wright (1993) looked at the purposes assigned to same-sex friendship among a large group of participants and reported that both women and men uniformly said that talk for talk's sake was the main purpose of meeting with friends. Engaging in joint tasks or activities was endorsed as the second main purpose, and meeting to deal with a specific relationship issue was mentioned third. Monsour (1992) also reported some interesting similarities in same-sex friendship after asking undergraduates to explain how they defined intimacy in their close friendships. Both women and men mentioned self-disclosure most frequently, followed by emotional expressiveness, support, physical contact, trust, and mutual activities, in declining order, indicating their definitions were quite similar. Gender similarities prevail in definitions of same-sex intimacy as well. Young women and men were equally likely to describe same-sex friendships as involving five dimensions: feeling appreciative of the friend, expressing it, feeling happiness, talking, and sharing activities (Helgeson et al., 1987). The two profiles described earlier show that gender similarities occur along most important friendship dimensions: Danielle and Kara, as well as Jamal and Steve, value the companionate aspects of the relationship very highly. In addition, both pairs rely mostly on conversation and common interests to sustain them, both know a great deal about each other's preferences and personal quirks, and both enjoy each other's company alone or in a group.

The conflicting interpretations described above indicate that there is not a simple answer to the question, "Do women's and men's friendships differ? Any answer should take at least four components into account, including: (1) what behaviors have been measured and how; (2) the degree of the difference; (3) individual differences, such as gender role identity and sexual orientation; and (4) situational variables, such as material resources, life stage, and cultural norms. First, gender differences may depend on what concepts or behaviors are used and how they are studied. For example, intimacy usually has been defined in feminine terms, that is, as including physical and verbal affection and self-disclosure (Cancian, 1987; Wood & Inman, 1993). This means that masculine ways of expressing closeness, such as washing a car or being a good provider, might be discounted. It also tends to disregard feminine instrumental acts, such as preparing a meal for someone or baby-sitting a sick friend's children.

Another important consideration concerning what behaviors are studied has to do with whether self-reports or actual observations are used. Women have been shown to disclose more than men in friendship, according to a meta-analysis of 205 studies conducted by Dindia and Allen (1992), most of which used self-report measures. However, at least one observational study of the conversations of same- and cross-sex friends done by Leaper and colleagues indicated that men were more self-disclosing in both same- and cross-sex friendships than women (Leaper, Carson, Baker, Holliday, & Myers, 1995). Women also were better listeners.

Second, gender differences in friendship may be less pronounced when the degree of difference between women and men is examined. For instance, in the Monsour (1992) study mentioned earlier, significantly more women than men listed self-disclosure as a meaning of intimacy, and more men than women listed shared activities. These results parallel conclusions that women are expressive and men are instrumental in friendship. However, a look at the degree of difference tempers this conclusion considerably. Self-disclosure was listed most often by both women and men (87% and 56%, respectively) and shared activities were ranked much lower by both (i.e., none of the women and only 9% of the men endorsed it). Thus, it is probably more accurate to conclude that both sexes value and define intimacy similarly in same-sex friendship, with differences being more a matter of degree than of substance. Likewise, Duck and Wright (1993) found that both women and men were quite positive about their same-sex friendships and that both described strong friendships as being instrumental *and* expressive, but women were even more positive about and expressive in their friendships than men.

Third, individual differences, including gender role identity or sexual orientation, sometimes have as much or more of an impact on friendship than gender. Young women and men who are androgynous (i.e., who perceive themselves as having a high number of both masculine and feminine traits) rate both the emotional and activity aspects of friendship more positively than do those who endorse traditional sex roles or who are undifferentiated (i.e., low in self-described feminine and masculine traits). They also report being more satisfied with their friendships and less lonely (Jones, Bloys, & Wood, 1990). Sexual orientation affects friendship, too. For lesbians and gay men, friendships often take on the roles usually provided by heterosexual families, partly to compensate for their family of origin's failure to acknowledge their identity (Weston, 1991). The effect of friends serving as extended family may mediate gender differences in friendship. In a study of 122 lesbians and 161 gay men, Nardi and Sherrod (1994) reported that lesbians and gay men seek emotional support equally from same-sex friends (excluding current lover). Similar levels of self-disclosure, social support, and participation in mutual activities also were found. A sexual component may enter into the same-sex friendships of lesbians and gay men, as well, whereas for heterosexuals, it is more likely to occur in cross-sex friendship. About half of both lesbians and gay men had sex at least once with their best friend in the past, but men were more likely than women to have had sex with close or casual friends. The extent to which sexual attraction affects same-sex friendships for bisexuals or even, perhaps, for some heterosexuals, has not been addressed.

Numerous situational variables also affect friendship, including access to material resources, dating or marital status, and cultural norms. Compared to women, men have more money and greater access to transportation. They also have more access to public space free from the fear of violence or harassment. Finally, they have more free time because traditionally they have less responsibility for child care (O'Connor, 1992). These resources make it easier for men to pursue friendships that rely on money, time, or public space, such as sports or going to a bar. However, women with similar resources might have friendship patterns more like men's.

Dating or marital status has an effect on both women's and men's friendships, but more so on women's. For example, Rose (1984) asked undergraduates to write an essay describing how a recent close or best same-sex friendship had ended. Four patterns of termination were identified. About 47% of the participants mentioned physical separation, such as moving to another city or school, as the primary reason the friendship ended, followed by learning something about the friend that led to dislike (e.g., violence, drug abuse, criticism) (22%), establishing new friendships that replaced the old (18%), and interference from dating or marital relationships (12%). Significantly more women (19%) than men (none) mentioned the last reason, dating or marriage, as affecting their friendships. Typical explanations were that the boyfriend did not like the woman's friend or that the woman preferred to spend time with her boyfriend rather than her friend. Complete the exercise in Figure 6.1 on *friendship lifelines* to explore further how friendships end.

This exercise is intended to help you understand changes in your friendship network. Use the chart below to indicate when each of your close same-sex friendships began and when (or if) they ended. As illustrated below, for each close or best friend you have had, draw a line indicating your age when the friendship started and a line to indicate when it ended, or alternatively, an arrow to indicate that the friendship is ongoing. Put the name or initials of each friend on the line representing that friendship.

Discussion Questions:
1. Look at the patterns of friendship formation and ending. To what do you attribute periods of high turnover (e.g., change of schools, high school graduation, getting married, and so forth)?
2. For each friendship that ended, write down the reason(s). Compare the reasons your adult same-sex friendships have ended with those of Rose (1984), reported in this chapter.
3. Ask a cross-sex friend to fill out a friendship lifeline and compare your reasons for ending the friendships. What gender differences do you observe, if any?
4. Fill out the friendship lifeline again focusing on close cross-sex friends. How few/many are there compared to same-sex friends? What periods of life were most conducive to cross-sex friendships?

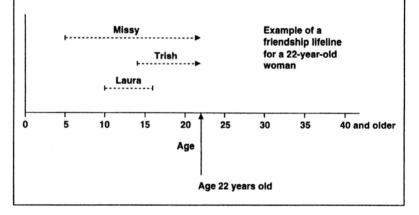

Figure 6.1. Friendship Lifeline

A cultural norm of homophobia in the United States (i.e., fear of homosexuality or homosexuals) has been argued to have a significant impact on same-sex friendship, particularly men's. Heterosexual men may avoid intimacy in friendships with men to avoid being perceived as homosexual (Nardi, 1992; Roese, Olson, Borenstein, Martin, & Shores, 1992). Support for this idea has been provided by Derlega and his colleagues, who investigated whether men are the special target of cultural prohibitions against physical affection in same-sex friendships (Derlega, Lewis, Harrison, Winstead, & Costanza, 1989). When pairs of actual friends were asked to act out how they would greet each other at the airport after returning from a trip, men friends were significantly less likely to hug or kiss each other than were women friends or cross-sex friends. In a separate study, it was also found that college students rated photographs of two men hugging or putting arms around each other's waist as significantly less normal than a picture with no touching between the men friends or ones showing two women or a woman and man hugging or with arms around each other's waist (Derlega et al., 1989). These results suggest that men may be less physically affectionate with same-sex friends due to a realistic concern that such behavior violates cultural norms.

In sum, research indicates that women's and men's best and close same-sex friendships probably are more similar than they are different, because differences *among* women or men are often more pronounced than differences *between* them. How a particular friendship operates may depend more on the two people's sex-role identity, material resources, dating status, and so on, than their gender. For instance, the same-sex friendships of single, androgynous, young women and men of similar economic means are likely to be highly similar, whereas those of older women or men who are married or have children, or who have traditional sex-role identities, may differ along more gender stereotypic lines. What differences there are tend to be concentrated in the areas of emotional expressiveness and responses to conflict. Even so, self-disclosure, help, loyalty, reciprocity, and commitment are likely to be valued in all same-sex friendships.

ъ Adult Cross-Sex Friendships

Shawna and Bill got to be friends after Shawna's friend, Marita, broke up with Bill. Before that, they had enjoyed each other's company but didn't get much chance to know each other. Shawna believed that

Marita didn't treat Bill right, but she would sometimes give him advice that would keep Marita interested in him. Bill appreciated Shawna's help, but, since the break-up, really has come to appreciate Shawna's wonderful sense of humor. They frequently watch prime-time television together one night a week alone or with other friends. Recently, Shawna started dating someone, so they haven't seen each other as much as usual.

Mark and Jana have been friends for 3 years. They originally dated for a while, but Jana decided she'd rather see someone else. They didn't run into each other for about 6 months, then ended up taking several of the same classes. They began to study together and now spend a few hours a week discussing their courses or their families and friends. Both Jana and Mark are dating someone, although Mark is still interested in dating Jana. The two couples double-dated a few times but didn't hit it off as a foursome, so now Jana and Mark usually just see each other after class.

Cross-sex friendships have been described as posing five challenges (O'Meara, 1989, 1994). The first is an *opportunity challenge*, referring to the fact that cross-sex friendships are less common than same-sex ones and are more difficult to establish. The opportunity challenge presented by cross-sex friendship has been supported by research. For instance, Rose (1985) found that young adults usually enact a specific strategy or script when forming a same-sex friendship (e.g., start by making plans to see the prospective friend, then, if all goes well, explore common interests or activities further). Few relied on same-sex friendships just happening. In contrast, three major means of establishing cross-sex friendships were described. First, 16% mentioned that knowing someone over time allowed the friendship to happen. Another one third said sexual attraction was the reason for initiating it; this strategy was never used in same-sex friendships. Last, one third of the adults indicated they had *no* strategy for forming cross-sex friendships. The friendship profiles described above illustrate the "just happened" approach to cross-sex friendship. In both, the woman and man came into contact repeatedly largely due to the context of the situation. Even though mutual liking was present, the friendship was not pursued deliberately outside this initial context until much later.

The opportunity challenge of cross-sex friendship is most easily overcome during young adulthood and by single adults. All the single undergraduates in the Rose (1985) study had at least one close cross-sex friend. Such relationships were less common among slightly older adults. All the single graduate men and 73% of the women also had a close cross-sex friend, but only 67% of married men and 53% of married women had a close cross-sex friend other than their spouse. According to Rawlins (1992), a male prerogative seems to be functioning once married; it is easier for men to initiate cross-sex friendships outside of marriage. In addition, when joint friendships with other couples are pursued, the prevailing pattern is for husbands to recruit the friends through work (e.g., Gerstel, 1988). In dual-career couples, the wife may play a stronger role in befriending couples.

The other four challenges described by O'Meara (1989) include (1) confronting the issue of sexuality, (2) determining the type of emotional bond the pair will have, (3) dealing with gender inequality in a relationship that values equality, and (4) presenting the relationship to the public. These issues are represented within the friendship profiles above. For instance, how the friends deal with Mark's sexual attraction is an ongoing issue in Jana and Mark's friendship. Shawna and Bill appear to have a stronger emotional bond than do Jana and Mark, who have made their friendship a lower priority than their romantic relationships, perhaps to more clearly present their friendship as being platonic to their dating partners and friends. In addition, Shawna and Bill have had to come to terms with certain gender inequalities in their relationship. At one point, Shawna felt that Bill was relying on her too much emotionally and that he was providing little in return in the friendship. Inequality has been less of a problem for Jana and Mark, who have focused their friendship almost exclusively on school work.

How formidable are these challenges for young adults' cross-sex friendships? Monsour, Harris, and Kurtzweil (1994) had participants answer this question by asking them whether these issues were present in their interactions with cross-sex friends during the past 3 weeks. The four challenges were a problem in some friendships, but not a majority. Issues related to the emotional bond were reported most frequently, followed by those concerning public image, sexuality, and equality, in declining frequency. Women were less likely to report problems surrounding sexuality than were men.

Cross-sex friendships also have been described as asymmetrical (Fehr, 1996; Rawlins, 1992). Men confide more in their best women friends than in their best men friends, and they spend more time with their best women friends and consult them more about significant decisions (e.g., Hacker, 1981). Men report giving less to, but being closer to and more intimate with, their women friends than their men friends, whereas the opposite is reported by women (Buhrke & Fuqua, 1987). Men also receive greater acceptance and intimacy in their cross-sex than same-sex friendships (Rose, 1985). In contrast, women obtain more acceptance and intimacy from women than men friends and indicate feeling happier more frequently in same-sex friendships (Helgeson et al., 1987; Rose, 1985). Only one friendship function, companionship, was more often provided to women by men friends (Rose, 1985).

Does the asymmetry of cross-sex friendships result in women being underbenefited in those relationships? It certainly appears that cross-sex friendships have the potential to re-create and reinforce inequitable gender roles. Snell, Belk, Flowers, and Warren (1988) reported that women were more likely to reveal feminine aspects of the self to men, such as how understanding they were, than masculine aspects, such as how outspoken they were. Men were more likely to reveal masculine behaviors than feminine ones. Likewise, when asked to write about what topics they would disclose to a friend, undergraduate women tended to select topics related to feminine content and men those related to masculine content (Derlega, Durham, Gockel, & Sholis, 1981). Hacker (1981) also found that women were more likely to reveal their weaknesses, and men their strengths, in cross-sex friendships. Similarly, Parks and Floyd (1996) found that women look to men friends significantly more often for help and advice, typical masculine domains, than men look to women friends for such assistance. Last, women describe friendships with men as being more patronizing, superficial, and sexist than men do (Sapadin, 1988).

Apparently, having a satisfying and equitable cross-sex friendship may be difficult to negotiate. One reason is that such relationships are relatively rare historically; a century ago they did not exist (Swain, 1992). As Western societies have become less gender segregated, opportunities for cross-sex friendships have increased. Women and men now are in the process of learning how to be friends. Research by Swain (1992) supports the idea that women and men can be adaptable in their friendship style. He found that men participants adopted a more self-disclosing style in cross-sex friendships than they used in same-sex ones, and women used a more masculine style of interaction with men friends than with women. Flexibility in women's and men's style of relating to different friends or under different conditions also has been reported (Reid & Fine, 1992; Reis, Senchak, & Solomon, 1985). These findings bode well for the future of cross-sex friendships.

Gender is not the only influence on cross-sex friendships. Individual differences and situational variables affect it, much as they do same-sex friendships. The cross-sex friendships of androgynous women and the same-sex friendships of androgynous men were found to be enhanced by their sex-role identity, because both groups emphasized the emotional and activity characteristics of friendship more positively than traditionally sex-typed or undifferentiated young adults (Jones et al., 1990). Sexual orientation also might affect the dynamics of cross-sex friendship. The sexual tensions in heterosexual cross-sex friendship presumably would be less likely in friendships between lesbians and gay men. Last, situational variables such as work or social class help to shape cross-sex friendships. Adult cross-sex friendships are primarily a middle-class phenomenon and are facilitated by occupational roles (Rubin, 1975). In fact, it is often crucial to career advancement to have cross-sex colleagues when in professional level jobs, particularly for women (Fine, 1986). Having friends at work, particularly male friends, also appears to be related to job satisfaction, at least among university faculty (Winstead, Derlega, Montgomery, & Pilkington, 1995).

Despite potential difficulties, several positive aspects of cross-sex friendship have been enumerated. Swain's (1992) participants indicated deriving pleasure from their cross-sex friendships that was not present in their same-sex relationships. Sapadin (1988) also reported that women and men appreciated the chance to see work and personal issues from the perspective of the other gender. As indicated earlier, men benefit from the emotional closeness that women friends provide. In turn, women often enjoy the companionship, lesser intensity, and status provided by male friends (Basow, 1992). In some situations, women feel more comfortable disclosing feelings like love to men friends than to women (Balswick, 1988). Platonic cross-sex friendships also have the ability to transcend modes of relating shaped by heterosexist scripts that routinely infuse sexuality into all interactions between women and men (Rawlins, 1994).

In general, cross-sex friendships are expected to increase and improve in the future, largely due to women's increased work roles. Work contexts that are most conducive to cross-sex friendships are those that are gender-integrated (as opposed to gender-segregated), include women and men of equal occupational status, support cross-sex friendships through the norms of the work environment, and promote formal and informal interactions between women and men (O'Meara, 1994). Werking (1994) also has pointed out that current research on cross-sex friendship is limited by a tendency always to contrast it with same-sex friendship. This comparative approach implies that cross-sex friendships are "deficient" relative to same-sex ones. She argues persuasively that it would be beneficial to our understanding of cross-sex friendship to treat it as a unique relationship, worthy of pursuit and study in its own right.

֍ Conclusions

Same- and cross-sex friendships are a significant part of the landscape of adult relationships. They provide a rich source of support, help, and companionship throughout the life cycle. Gender affects friendship in some systematic ways, particularly by defining what activities and values govern friendships for same-sex groups in childhood. Gender differences that are observed in adulthood include greater intimacy and affection among women friends and a greater emphasis on shared activities among men friends. Same-sex friendships share a number of similarities as well. Both women and men define intimacy as including self-disclosure, sharing activities, and feeling and expressing appreciation for the friend.

Gender appears to affect cross-sex friendships more strongly, particularly for heterosexuals. Adults' strategies for forming cross-sex friendships are less well-developed than those for pursuing same-sex friends. Once a cross-sex friendship has taken root, there are other challenges to the relationship, including sexual attraction, expressing affection, gender inequality, and public perceptions of the friendship.

Other factors often have been shown to shape friendships more profoundly than gender alone. Life stage, gender-role identity, sexual orientation, and material resources may influence both same- and cross-sex friendships more than gender, indicating that differences among women and men may be more significant than differences *between* them. For instance, a traditionally feminine woman college student might have friendships quite different from those of an androgynous lesbian student or of an older single professional woman. Thus, solely knowing someone's gender does not allow one to accurately predict what her or his friendships would be like.

As changes in women's and men's social circumstances and roles continue, the vistas of friendship are likely to expand. Women's and men's same-sex friendships probably will become more similar as androgynous gender roles become more acceptable. Already, men are seeking closer ties in their friendships and women are engaging in more group activities such as sports with friends (Ivy & Backlund, 1994). Women and men also are learning to relate more effectively to each other. Cross-sex friendships should benefit from improved communication as well as from workplace contact, which allows men and women to overcome the opportunity challenge of cross-sex friendships. Overall, the future of friendship seems quite promising.

7

Epilogue
Final Thoughts

I n the end, given all the theory and research and thinking and
writing that social scientists have invested their time and energy in, what can we really say about gender and relationships?
Did the studies reviewed in previous chapters confirm your expectations about how women and men differ in their relationships?
Were there some outcomes you expected and some that were
surprising to you? Do you find evidence of gender differences in
relationships reassuring, or do you wish they would disappear?
Did you think of questions that were not addressed by the research
reviewed in this book?

   In this final chapter, we want to look again at the theories of
gender that we started with in Chapter 1 and see how they fare in
the context of the research on gender and relationships. We also

want to comment on doing research on gender and relationships and suggest some ways that you or others can contribute to this literature. Finally, we want to think about the implications of the information in this book for our real-life relationships.

✦ Theories Revisited

Theories of gender differences in relationships were organized in terms of two dimensions: structural versus individual and socialization versus biology. Perhaps because of our belief that we can control our fate, psychological research tends to emphasize the individual approach to the study of relationships. Think about the studies described in the book. Most use the individual participant as a reporter on his or her relationship attitudes, feelings, and behaviors. The focus of these studies is generally on what characteristics of the *individual*, including gender, affect these relationship variables. We find, however, that structural variables (aspects of the relationship outside of the individual) are also important. For example, in Chapter 4, we reported that having children "traditionalizes" the division of family work. Couples that may have adopted a share-and-share-alike approach to doing household chores tend to view child care responsibilities as belonging to the woman. As she takes on caretaking tasks, she may find herself doing more of the other household work, until the division of family work is no longer balanced. As described in Chapter 4, this imbalance affects her relationship satisfaction and perhaps conflict in the relationship as well.

The relatively small number of examples of the influence of structural variables in the book is due not to their unimportance but to our choosing to review research primarily from psychology rather than other disciplines (e.g., sociology) where these variables are more likely to be studied. It is also the case that gender has been treated more often as an individual variable (using an individual's femaleness or maleness as a variable) rather than a structural variable (using responses to or expectations of femaleness or maleness as a variable).

Another way that external variables affect the interplay between gender and relationships is through the influence of social class, religion, and culture. Religions, through their interpreters (i.e., religious leaders and clerics), usually specify how women and men should and should not interact. Social and cultural traditions also mold relationships. For example, in the United States, most women change their surname to their husband's when they marry. Historically this name change was enforced by law because a woman's identity and property became legally incorporated into her husband's upon marriage. Although a woman's legal status is no longer secondary to a man's, the tradition of changing names continues. In what ways does this tradition influence a woman and man entering into a marital relationship? In many Asian cultures, arranged marriages or marriages requiring clear parental approval are the norm. In these cultures there tends to be less emphasis on individual choice and the importance of romantic feelings and more on family obligations and the welfare of the family. Although valuing of family over individual affects both females and males, it may affect them differently (Dion & Dion, 1993).

Cultural expectations for female and male behavior may also influence friendships. In many countries (e.g., India, Egypt, China), expressions of physical affection between men are common. Male friends hug and hold hands, and these behaviors are not regarded as indications of romantic or sexual feelings as they might be in the United States. Berman, Murphy-Berman, and Pachauri (1988) studied best same-sex friendships in India and the United States and found larger gender differences in the United States than in India. Similarly, Wheeler, Reis, and Bond (1989) found no difference in self-disclosure among Chinese students in Hong Kong despite finding that females students in the United States reported higher levels of disclosure than their male counterparts. Psychologists are becoming increasingly interested in the impact of culture on relationships, but as these examples illustrate, investigations of the interaction between culture and gender are also needed.

Because psychological research is most likely to focus on individuals, then the second dimension: socialization versus biology is the most frequently used in this book. The most popular biological explanation, well illustrated in Chapter 2, "Attraction and Dating," and Chapter 3, "Sexual Relations," is evolutionary psychology. This approach assumes that women and men behave differently in relationships because their reproductive success requires different mating strategies. Although evolutionary explanations are difficult to disconfirm, there is also ample evidence of socializing forces at work. It is interesting, too, that evolutionary psychology has thus far focused primarily on romantic and sexual relationships rather than friendships. As Chapter 6, "Friendship," argues, gender socialization and gender segregation contribute to the development of differences in girls' and boys' relationships with their friends. The social skills and expectations learned in same-sex friendships may also influence the development of romantic relationships. The debate about the relative impact of biological versus socialization factors on gender differences will continue.

❧ Research on Gender and Relationships

The book has reviewed large numbers of studies but has given relatively little guidance concerning future research. We hope that some of our readers will want not only to learn about gender and relationships but also to contribute to this topic by conducting research. Considering the research that has already been done, we have these suggestions:

1. Get beyond self-reports. Too much of the research simply asks participants to report on their attitudes, feelings, wishes, or expectations. These self-reports, no matter how honest and accurate, may not reflect what participants actually *do*. For example, as reported in Chapter 2, men's preferences for beauty in a marriage partner are stronger than women's, and women's preferences for economic resources in a marriage partner are stronger than men's, but Stevens et al. (1990) found that, beyond a matching effect, more beautiful women do not marry more successful men and more successful men do not marry more beautiful women. Thus, women and men do not or cannot, in fact, capitalize on their preferred asset and exchange it for what they say they want in a heterosexual partner.

Self-reports of actual behaviors are very often used. In some cases, that is, sexual behavior, we have no choice but to use participants' own reports. In others, such as self-disclosure and verbal and nonverbal behavior during marital conflict, we can observe and code the actual behavior. Behavior recorded in a laboratory setting may also be a less than perfect reflection of what goes on outside of the lab. As pointed out in Chapter 6, self-reports and ratings of actual behavior do not always yield the same results. We should place more weight on those measures that most closely approximate real behavior in real relationships; and research needs to seek ways to gather data on real behavior in real relationships.

2. *Get beyond observations of gender differences.* Too often the point of a study seems to be simply that girls and boys or women and men are different. The introductory chapter should have steered you away from attempting to find out definitively *why* gender differences occur, but there is plenty of opportunity to find out when, under what circumstances, or for which types of participants gender differences occur. Earlier in this chapter, we mentioned that religion, ethnicity, and culture might influence the extent of gender differences. In several chapters, age and stage of relationship have been shown to influence gender differences. Because so many research projects have been done with predominantly white and middle-class college students, our understanding of normative relationship behaviors may be wrong for individuals from other ethnic groups or social classes or for nonstudents or for older persons.

All of the topics covered in the book are incomplete in terms of our understanding of them. We hope that for many of you, the studies reviewed here will inspire you to improve on what has been done, to pursue explanations that have been inadequately researched, and to ask new questions in the area of gender and relationships.

⚓ Implications for Your Relationships

As the research indicates, most of us want relationships with partners who are kind, understanding, intelligent and have an exciting personality. We want romantic relationships and friendships that are intimate and emotionally satisfying. Most of us want romantic or marital/partnered relationships that are sexually satisfying. It is also true that we need relationship partners who can help us accomplish and deal with life's everyday tasks, especially family work. Do gender differences, gender roles, gender scripts help us reach these goals or hurt us?

Recent books by Schwartz (1995), *Love Between Equals: How Peer Marriages Really Work,* and Rivers and Barnett (1996), *She Works/He Works: How Two-Income Families Are Happier, Healthier, and Better-Off,* present evidence of the advantages of equal partnerships in marriage. Gender scripts and gender roles that set expectations for what women and men can/will/should do in a relationship are barriers to equality. Expecting the man to initiate a relationship or to move a relationship from a platonic to a sexual plane restricts both his role in the relationship and hers. Expecting the woman to be the primary caretaker for young children sets limits on the kind of relationships that the man will have with the children and sets limits on the woman's opportunities to assume other roles in life. As pointed out in Chapter 1, roles are also training grounds for personal characteristics. An initiator must be assertive, persistent, even aggressive. A caretaker must be interpersonally sensitive, responsive, even self-martyring.

In ongoing relationships, we often find that we wish our partner were more of "this" and less of "that." But have they had the opportunity, and have you given them the opportunity, to display or acquire those characteristics? You want your boyfriend or husband to remember your birthday, but who takes responsibility for remembering all other birthdays in your family or social network? You want your girlfriend or wife to be more decisive, to make up her mind, but who takes responsibility for making important plans or has unilateral power to change plans if something comes up?

But, you say, I like women who are sensitive or men who are decisive. Ickes (1993) has discussed the paradox that although we may be initially attracted to women or men with traditional gender roles, even strongly so, we may not fare well in ongoing relationships with these individuals. Masculine men and feminine women may match our romantic ideal, but in dealing with everyday stresses and the unavoidable demands and conflicts of an intimate relationship, men who can be caring and sensitive as well as masculine and women who can be autonomous and assertive as well as feminine may actually make better life partners.

References

Abbey, A. (1982). Sex differences in attributions for friendly behavior: Do males misperceive females' friendliness? *Journal of Personality and Social Psychology, 42,* 830-838.

Abbey, A. (1991). Misperception as an antecedent of acquaintance rape: A consequence of ambiguity in communication between women and men. In A. Parrot & L. Bechhofer (Eds.), *Acquaintance rape: The hidden crime* (pp. 96-111). New York: John Wiley.

Acitelli, L. K. (1992). Gender differences in relationships awareness and marital satisfaction among young married couples. *Personality and Social Psychology Bulletin, 18,* 102-110.

Acitelli, L. K., & Antonucci, T. C. (1994). Gender differences in the link between marital support and satisfaction in older couples. *Journal of Personality and Social Psychology, 67,* 688-698.

Antill, J. K. (1987). Parents' beliefs and values about sex roles, sex differences, and sexuality: Their sources and implications. In P. Shaver & C. Hendrick (Eds.), *Sex and gender* (pp. 294-328). Newbury Park, CA: Sage.

Antioch College. (1992). *The Antioch College sexual offense policy approved by the Board of Trustees in June 1992.* (Available from Antioch College, 795 Livermore Street, Yellow Springs, OH 45387)

Argyle, M., & Henderson, M. (1984). The rules of friendship. *Journal of Social and Personal Relationships, 1,* 211-237.

Babcock, J. S., Waltz, J., Jacobson, N. S., & Gottman, J. M. (1993). Power and violence: The relation between communication patterns, power discrepancies, and domestic violence. *Journal of Consulting and Clinical Psychology, 61,* 40-50.

Balswick, J. (1988). *The inexpressive male.* Lexington, MA: Lexington Books.

Bank, B. (1994). Effects of national, school, and gender cultures on friendships among adolescents in Australia and the United States. *Youth and Society, 25,* 435-456.

Barnard, G. W., Vera, M., & Newman, G. (1982). "Till death do us part": A study of spouse murder. *Bulletin of the American Academy of Psychiatry and Law, 10,* 271-280.

Barnett, R. C., & Baruch, G. K. (1987). Determinants of fathers' participation in family work. *Journal of Marriage and the Family, 49,* 29-40.

Basow, S. A. (1992). *Gender: Stereotypes and roles.* Pacific Grove, CA: Brooks/Cole.

Baumeister, R. F., Smart, L., & Boden, J. M. (1996). Relation of threatened egotism to violence and aggression: The dark side of high self-esteem. *Psychological Review, 103,* 5-33.

Baxter, L. A., & Dindia, K. (1990). Marital partners' perceptions of maintenance strategies. *Journal of Social and Personal Relationships, 7,* 187-209.

Belsky, J. (1990). Children and marriage. In F. D. Fincham & T. N. Bradbury (Eds.), *The psychology of marriage* (pp. 172-200). New York: Guilford.

Bem, S. L. (1981). Gender schema theory: A cognitive account of sex typing. *Psychological Review, 88,* 354-364.

Bem, S. L. (1993). *The lenses of gender: Transforming the debate on sexual inequality.* New Haven, CT: Yale University Press.

Bem, S. L., & Lenney, E. (1976). Sex-typing and the avoidance of cross-sex behavior. *Journal of Personality and Social Psychology, 33,* 48-54.

Berman, J. J., Murphy-Berman, V., & Pachauri, A. (1988). Sex differences in friendship patterns in India and in the United States. *Basic and Applied Social Psychology, 9,* 61-71.

Bettor, L., Hendrick, S. S., & Hendrick, C. (1995). Gender and sexual standards in dating relationships. *Personal Relationships, 2,* 359-369.

Biernat, M., & Wortman, C. B. (1991). Sharing of home responsibilities between professionally employed women and their husbands. *Journal of Personality and Social Psychology, 60,* 844-860.

Bigelow, B. J., & LaGaipa, J. J. (1980). The development of friendship values and choice. In H. C. Foot, A. J. Chapman, & J. R. Smith (Eds.), *Friendship and social relations in children* (pp. 15-44). Chichester, UK: John Wiley.

Blair, S. L., & Lichter, D. T. (1991). Measuring the division of household labor: Gender segregation of housework among American couples. *Journal of Family Issues, 12,* 91-113.

Blumstein, P. W., & Schwartz, P. (1983). *American couples.* New York: William Morrow.

Blumstein, P. W., & Schwartz, P. (1991). Money and ideology: Their impact on power and the division of household labor. In R. L. Blumberg (Ed.), *Gender, family, and economy: The triple overlap* (pp. 261-288). Newbury Park, CA: Sage.

Brehm, S. S. (1992). *Intimate relationships.* New York: McGraw-Hill.

Brown, L. S. (1995). Therapy with same-sex couples: An introduction. In N. S. Jacobson & A. S. Gurman (Eds.), *Clinical handbook of couple therapy* (pp. 274-291). New York: Guilford.

Brown, M., & Auerback, A. (1981). Communication patterns in initiation of marital sex. *Medical Aspects of Human Sexuality, 15,* 235-254.

Buhrke, R., & Fuqua, D. (1987). Sex differences in same- and cross-sex supportive relationships. *Sex Roles, 17,* 339-352.

Burnett, R. (1987). Reflections in personal relationships. In R. Burnett, P. McGhee, & D. D. Clarke (Eds.), *Accounting for relationships: Explanation, representation, and knowledge* (pp. 74-93). London: Methuen.

Buss, D. M. (1988). The evolution of human intrasexual competition: Tactics of mate attraction. *Journal of Personality and Social Psychology, 54,* 616-628.

Buss, D. M. (1989). Sex differences in human mate preferences: Evolutionary hypotheses tested in 37 cultures. *Behavioral and Brain Sciences, 12,* 1-49.

Buss, D. M. (1991). Evolutionary personality psychology. *Annual Review of Psychology, 42,* 459-491.

Buss, D. M., & Barnes, M. (1986). Preferences in human mate selection. *Journal of Personality and Social Psychology, 50,* 559-570.

Buss, D. M., & Schmitt, D. P. (1993). Sexual strategies theory: An evolutionary perspective on human mating. *Psychological Review, 100,* 204-232.

Canary, D. J., Cupach, W. R., & Messman, S. J. (1995). *Relationship conflict: Conflict in parent-child, friendship, and romantic relationships.* Thousand Oaks, CA: Sage.

Canary, D. J., & Stafford, L. (1992). Relational maintenance strategies and equity in marriage. *Communication Monographs, 59,* 239-267.

Cancian, F. M. (1987). The feminization of love. *Signs: Journal of Women in Culture and Society, 11,* 692-709.

Cascardi, M., Langhinrichsen, J., & Vivian, D. (1992). Marital aggression: Impact, injury, and health correlates for husbands and wives. *Archives of Internal Medicine, 152,* 1178-1184.

Catania, J. A., Coates, T. J., & Kegeles, S. (1994). A test of the AIDS risk reduction model: Psychosocial correlates of condom use in the AMEN cohort study. *Health Psychology, 13,* 548-555.

Cate, R. M., Long, E., Angera, J. J., & Draper, K. K. (1993). Sexual intercourse and relationship development. *Family Relations, 42,* 158-164.

Chodorow, N. (1978). *The reproduction of mothering: Psychoanalysis and the sociology of gender.* Berkeley: University of California Press.

Christensen, A. (1988). Dysfunctional interaction patterns in couples. In P. Noller & M. A. Fitzpatrick (Eds.), *Perspectives on marital interaction* (pp. 31-52). Clevedon, UK: Multilingual Matters.

Christensen, A., & Heavey, C. L. (1993). Gender differences in marital conflict: The demand/withdraw interaction pattern. In S. Oskamp & M. Costanzo (Eds.), *Gender issues in contemporary society* (pp. 113-140). Newbury Park, CA: Sage.

Christensen, A., & Shenk, J. L. (1991). Communication, conflict, and psychological distance in nondistressed, clinic, and divorcing couples. *Journal of Consulting and Clinical Psychology, 59,* 458-463.

Clark, M. L., & Ayers, M. (1993). Friendship expectations and friendship evaluations: Reciprocity and gender effects. *Youth and Society, 24,* 299-313.

Clark, R. D., III. (1990). The impact of AIDS on gender differences in willingness to engage in casual sex. *Journal of Applied Social Psychology, 20,* 771-782.

Clark, R. D., III, & Hatfield, E. (1989). Gender differences in receptivity to sexual offers. *Journal of Psychology and Human Sexuality, 2,* 39-55.

Cline, R. J. W., & McKenzie, N. J. (1994). Sex differences in communication and the construction of HIV/AIDS. *Journal of Applied Communication Research, 22,* 322-337.

Crosby, F. J. (1991). *Juggling.* New York: Free Press.

Crouter, A. C., Perry-Jenkins, M., Huston, T. L., & McHale, S. M. (1987). Processes underlying father involvement in dual-earner and single-earner families. *Developmental Psychology, 23,* 431-440.

Cupach, W. R., & Canary, D. J. (1995). Managing conflict and anger: Investigating the sex stereotype hypothesis. In P. J. Kalbfleisch & M. J. Cody (Eds.), *Gender, power, and communication in human relationships* (pp. 233-252). Hillsdale, NJ: Lawrence Erlbaum.

Dabbs, J. M., Ruback, R. B., & Besch, N. F. (1987). *Male saliva testosterone following conversations with male and female partners.* Convention poster, American Psychological Association, New York.

Dainton, K., & Baxter, L. A. (1993). Routine maintenance behaviors: A comparison of relationship type, partner similarity, and sex differences. *Journal of Social and Personal Relationships, 10,* 255-271.

Dainton, K., & Stafford, L. (1993). Routine maintenance behaviors: A comparison of relationship type, partner similarity, and sex differences. *Journal of Social and Personal Relationships, 10,* 255-271.

Darling, C. A., Davidson, J. K., Sr., & Passarelo, L. C. (1992). The mystique of first intercourse among college youth: The role of partners, contraceptive practices, and psychological reactions. *Journal of Youth and Adolescence, 21,* 97-117.

DeLamater, J. (1987). Gender differences in sexual scenarios. In K. Kelley (Ed.), *Females, males, and sexuality: Theories and research* (pp. 127-140). Albany: SUNY Press.

Derlega, V. J., Durham, B., Gockel, B., & Sholis, D. (1981). Sex differences in self-disclosure: Effects of topic content, friendship, and partner's sex. *Sex Roles, 7*, 433-447.

Derlega, V. J., Lewis, R. J., Harrison, S., Winstead, B. A., & Costanza, R. (1989). Gender differences in the initiation and attribution of tactile intimacy. *Journal of Nonverbal Behavior, 13*, 83-96.

Dindia, K. (1994). A multiphasic view of relationship maintenance strategies. In D. J. Canary & L. Stafford (Eds.), *Communication and relational maintenance* (pp. 91-112). San Diego: Academic Press.

Dindia, K., & Allen, M. (1992). Sex differences in self-disclosure: A metaanalysis. *Psychological Bulletin, 112*, 106-124.

Dindia, K., & Baxter, L. A. (1987). Strategies for maintaining and repairing marital relationships. *Journal of Social and Personal Relationships, 4*, 143-158.

Dion, K. K., & Dion, K. L. (1993). Individualistic and collectivistic perspectives on gender and the cultural context of love and intimacy. *Journal of Social Issues, 49*, 53-69.

Dittman, R. W., Kappes, M. H., Kappes, M. E., Borger, D., Stegner, H., Willig, R. H., & Wallis, H. (1990). Congenital adrenal hyperplasia I: Gender-related behavior and attitudes in female patients and sisters. *Psychoneuroendocrinology, 15*, 401-420.

Douvan, E. (1983). Commentary: Theoretical perspectives on peer association. In J. L. Epstein & N. Karweit (Eds.), *Friends in school: Patterns of selection and influence in secondary schools* (pp. 63-69). New York: Academic Press.

Draper, P., & Belsky, J. (1990). Personality development in evolutionary perspective. *Journal of Personality, 58*, 141-161.

Duck, S. (1991). *Understanding relationships.* New York: Guilford.

Duck, S., & Wright, P. H. (1993). Reexamining gender differences in same-gender friendships: A close look at two kinds of data. *Sex Roles, 28*, 709-727.

Eagly, A. H. (1987). *Sex differences in social behavior: A social-role interpretation.* Hillsdale, NJ: Lawrence Erlbaum.

Eagly, A. H., & Steffen, V. J. (1984). Gender stereotypes stem from the distribution of women and men into social roles. *Journal of Personality and Social Psychology, 46*, 735-754.

Eagly, A. H., & Wood, W. (1982). Inferred sex differences in status as a determinant of gender stereotypes about social influence. *Journal of Personality and Social Psychology, 43*, 915-928.

Ehrhardt, A. A., & Meyer-Bahlburg, H. F. L. (1981). Effects of prenatal sex hormones on gender-related behavior. *Science, 211*, 1312-1318.

Eisler, R., & Skidmore, J. (1987). Masculine gender role stress: Scale development and component factors in the appraisal of stressful situations. *Behavior Modification, 11,* 123-136.

Epstein, J. L. (1986). Friendship selection: Development and environmental influences. In E. C. Mueller & C. R. Cooper (Eds.), *Process and outcome in peer relationships* (pp. 129-160). New York: Academic Press.

Eshel, Y., & Kurman, J. (1990). Love is not enough: Determinants of adolescent preference for other-sex and same-sex peers. *British Journal of Developmental Psychology, 8,* 171-178.

Faulkenberry, J. R., Vincent, M., James, A., & Johnson, W. (1987). Coital behaviors, attitudes, and knowledge of students who experience early coitus. *Adolescence, 22,* 321-332.

Fehr, B. (1996). *Friendship processes.* Thousand Oaks, CA: Sage.

Feingold, A. (1990). Gender differences in effects of physical attractiveness on romantic attraction: A comparison across five research paradigms. *Journal of Personality and Social Psychology, 59,* 981-993.

Feld, S. L., & Straus, M. A. (1990). Escalation and desistance from wife assault in marriage. In M. A. Straus & R. J. Gelles (Eds.), *Physical violence in American families: Risk factors and adaptations to violence in 8,145 families* (pp. 489-505). New Brunswick, NJ: Transaction Books.

Ferree, M. M. (1987). She works hard for a living: Gender and class on the job. In B. B. Hess & M. M. Ferree (Eds.), *Analyzing gender: A handbook of social science research* (pp. 322-347). Newbury Park, CA: Sage.

Ferree, M. M. (1991). The gender division of labor in two-earner marriages. *Journal of Family Issues, 12,* 158-180.

Fine, G. A. (1986). Friendships in the workplace. In V. J. Derlega & B. A. Winstead (Eds.), *Friendship and social interaction* (pp. 185-206). New York: Springer-Verlag.

Fish, L. S., New, R. S., & Van Cleave, N. J. (1992). Shared parenting in dual-income families. *American Journal of Orthopsychiatry, 62,* 83-92.

Fisher, J. D., & Fisher, W. A. (1990). [College students predictive study of AIDS risk reduction]. Unpublished raw data. Cited in S. S. Williams, D. Kimble, N. H. Covell, L. H. Weiss, K. J. Newton, J. D. Fisher, & W. A. Fisher. (1992). College students use implicit personality theory instead of safer sex. *Journal of Applied Social Psychology, 22,* 921-933.

Fitzpatrick, M. A. (1987). Marriage and verbal intimacy. In V. J. Derlega & J. H. Berg (Eds.), *Self-disclosure: Theory, research, and therapy* (pp. 131-154). New York: Plenum.

Fitzpatrick, M. A. (1988). *Between husbands and wives: Communication in marriage.* Newbury Park, CA: Sage.

Frable, D. E. S. (1989). Sex typing and gender ideology: Two facets of the individual's gender psychology that go together. *Journal of Personality and Social Psychology, 56,* 95-108.

Frable, D. E. S., & Bem, S. L. (1985). If you're gender-schematic, all members of the opposite sex look alike. *Journal of Personality and Social Psychology, 49,* 459-468.

Furman, W., & Bierman, K. L. (1984). Children's conceptions of friendship: A multimethod study of developmental changes. *Developmental Psychology, 20,* 925-931.

Gagnon, J. H., & Simon, W. (1973). *Sexual conduct: The social sources of human sexuality.* Chicago, IL: Aldine.

Galligan, R. F., & Terry, D. J. (1993). Romantic ideals, fear of negative implications, and the practice of safe sex. *Journal of Applied Social Psychology, 23,* 1685-1711.

Gerstel, N. (1988). Divorce, gender, and social integration. *Gender and Society, 2,* 343-363.

Gilmore, D. D. (1990). *Manhood in the making: Cultural concepts of masculinity.* New Haven, CT: Yale University Press.

Gold, R. S., Skinner, M. J., & Ross, M. W. (1994). Unprotected anal intercourse in HIV-infected and non-HIV infected gay men. *Journal of Sex Research, 31,* 59-77.

Gonzales, M. H., & Meyers, S. A. (1993). "Your mother would like me": Self-presentation in the personals ads of heterosexual and homosexual men and women. *Personality and Social Psychology Bulletin, 19,* 131-142.

Gottman, J. M. (1993). The roles of conflict engagement, escalation, and avoidance in marital interaction: A longitudinal view of five types of couples. *Journal of Consulting and Clinical Psychology, 61,* 6-15.

Gottman, J. M. (1994). *What predicts divorce? The relationship between marital processes and marital outcomes.* Hillsdale, NJ: Lawrence Erlbaum.

Gottman, J. M., & Krokoff, L. J. (1989). Marital interaction and satisfaction: A longitudinal view. *Journal of Consulting and Clinical Psychology, 57,* 47-52.

Gottman, J. M., & Levenson, R. W. (1986). Assessing the role of emotion in marriage. *Behavioral Assessment, 8,* 31-48.

Gottman, J. M., & Levenson, R. W. (1992). Marital processes predictive of later dissolution: Behavior, physiology, and health. *Journal of Personality and Social Psychology, 63,* 221-233.

Gottman, J. M., Markman, H., & Notarius, C. (1977). The topography of marital conflict: A sequential analysis of verbal and nonverbal behavior. *Journal of Marriage and the Family, 39,* 461-478.

Green, B. L., & Kenrick, D. T. (1994). The attractiveness of gender-typed traits at different relationship levels: Androgynous characteristics may be desirable after all. *Personality and Social Psychology Bulletin, 20,* 244-253.

Grote, N. K., Frieze, I. B., & Stone, C. A. (1996). Children, traditionalism in the division of family work, and marital satisfaction: "What's love got to do with it?" *Personal Relationships, 3,* 211-228.

Hacker, H. (1981). Blabbermouths and clams: Sex differences in self-disclosure in same-sex and cross-sex friendship dyads. *Psychology of Women Quarterly, 5*, 385-401.

Hartup, W. W. (1996). The company they keep: Friendships and their developmental significance. *Child Development, 67*, 1-13.

Hatfield, E., Sprecher, S., Pillermer, J. T., Greenberger, D., & Wexler, P. (1988). Gender differences in what is desired in the sexual relationship. *Journal of Psychology and Human Sexuality, 1*, 39-52.

Heavey, C. L., Christensen, A., & Malamuth, N. M. (1995). The longitudinal impact of demand and withdrawal during marital conflict. *Journal of Consulting and Clinical Psychology, 63*, 797-801.

Heavey, C. L., Layne, C., & Christensen, A. (1993). Gender and conflict structure in marital interaction: A replication and extension. *Journal of Consulting and Clinical Psychology, 61*, 16-27.

Helgeson, V. S., Shaver, P., & Dyer, M. (1987). Prototypes of intimacy and distance in same-sex and opposite-sex relationships. *Journal of Social and Personal Relationships, 4*, 195-233.

Hendrick, S. S. (1981). Self-disclosure and marital satisfaction. *Journal of Personality and Social Psychology, 40*, 1150-1159.

Herzfeld, M. (1985). *The poetics of manhood: Contest and identity in a Cretan mountain village.* Princeton, NJ: Princeton University Press.

Himadi, W. G., Arkowitz, H., Hinton, R., & Perl, J. (1980). Minimal dating and its relationship to other social problems and general adjustment. *Behavior Therapy, 11*, 345-352.

Hines, M. (1982). Prenatal gonadal hormones and sex differences in human behavior. *Psychological Bulletin, 92*, 56-80.

Hochschild, A. (1989). *The second shift.* New York: Viking.

Holtzworth-Munroe, A., Waltz, J., Jacobson, N. S., Monaco, V., Fehrenbach, P. A., & Gottman, J. M. (1992). Recruiting nonviolent men as control subjects for research on marital violence. How easily can it be done? *Violence and Victims, 7*, 79-88.

Hunt, M. (1974). *Sexual behavior in the 1970s.* Chicago: Playboy Press.

Huston, T. L., & Ashmore, R. D. (1986). Women and men in personal relationships. In R. D. Ashmore & F. K. Del Boca (Eds.), *The social psychology of female-male relations* (pp. 167-210). Orlando, FL: Academic Press.

Huston, T. L., Surra, C. A., Fitzgerald, N. M., & Cate, R. M. (1981). From courtship to marriage: Mate selection as an interpersonal process. In S. Duck & R. Gilmour (Eds.), *Personal relationships 2: Developing personal relationships* (pp. 53-88). San Diego, CA: Academic Press.

Ickes, W. (1993). Traditional gender roles: Do they make, and then break, our relationships? *Journal of Social Issues, 49*(3), 71-86.

Island, D., & Letellier, P. (1991). *Men who beat the men who love them: Battered gay men and domestic violence.* New York: Haworth.

Ivy, D. K., & Backlund, P. (1994). *Exploring genderspeak*. New York: McGraw-Hill.

Jacobson, N. S., Gottman, J. M., Waltz, J., Rushe, R., Babcock, J., & Holtzworth-Munroe, A. (1994). Affect, verbal content, and psychophysiology in the arguments of couples with a violent husband. *Journal of Consulting and Clinical Psychology, 62*, 982-988.

Johnson, M. P. (1995). Patriarchal terrorism and common couple violence: Two forms of violence against women. *Journal of Marriage and the Family, 57*, 283-294.

Jones, D. C., Bloys, N., & Wood, M. (1990). Sex roles and friendship patterns. *Sex Roles, 23*, 133-145.

Josephs, R. A., Markus, H. R., & Tafarodi, R. W. (1992). Gender and self-esteem. *Journal of Personality and Social Psychology, 63*, 391-402.

Julien, D., & Markman, H. J. (1991). Social support and social networks as determinants of individual and marital outcomes. *Journal of Social and Personal Relationships, 8*, 549-568.

Julien, D., Markman, H. J., & Lindahl, K. (1989). A comparison of a global and a microanalytic coding system: Implications for future trends in studying interactions. *Behavioral Assessment, 11*, 81-100.

Karney, B. R., & Bradbury, T. N. (1995). The longitudinal course of marital quality and stability: A review of theory, method, and research. *Psychological Bulletin, 118*, 3-34.

Kelly, C., Huston, T. L., & Cate, R. M. (1985). Premarital relationship correlates of the erosion of satisfaction in marriage. *Journal of Social and Personal Relationships, 2*, 167-178.

Kelly, J. A., Kalichman, S. C., Kauth, M. R., Kilgore, H. G., Hood, H. V., Campos, P. E., Rao, S. M., Brasfield, T. L., & St. Lawrence, J. S. (1991). Situational factors associated with AIDS risk behavior lapses and coping strategies used by gay men who successfully avoid lapses. *Journal of Public Health, 81*, 1335-1338.

Kenrick, D. T. (1994). Evolutionary social psychology: From sexual selection to social cognition. In M. P. Zanna (Ed.), *Advances in experimental social psychology* (Vol. 26, pp. 75-121). San Diego, CA: Academic Press.

Kenrick, D. T., Groth, G. E., Trost, M. R., & Sadalla, E. K. (1993). Integrating evolutionary and social exchange perspectives on relationships: Effects of gender, self-appraisal, and involvement level on mate selection criteria. *Journal of Personality and Social Psychology, 64*, 951-969.

Kirkpatrick, L. A., & Davis, K. E. (1994). Attachment style, gender, and relationships stability: A longitudinal analysis. *Journal of Personality and Social Psychology, 66*, 502-512.

Klinkenberg, D., & Rose, S. (1994). Dating scripts of gay men and lesbians. *Journal of Homosexuality, 26*(4), 23-35.

Knox, D., & Wilson, K. (1981). Dating behaviors of university students. *Family Relations, 30*, 255-258.

Koss, M. P., Dinero, T. E., & Seibel, C. A. (1988). Stranger and acquaintance rape: Are there differences in the victim's experience? *Psychology of Women Quarterly, 12,* 1-24.

Koss, M. P., Gidycz, C. A., & Wisniewski, N. (1987). The scope of rape: Incidence and prevalence of sexual aggression and victimization in a national sample of higher education students. *Journal of Consulting and Clinical Psychology, 55,* 162-170.

Koss, M. P., Goodman, L. A., Browne, A., Fitzgerald, L. F., Keita, G. P., & Russo, N. F. (1994). *No safe haven: Male violence against women at home, at work, and in the community.* Washington, DC: American Psychological Association.

Kurdek, L. (1989). Relationship quality in gay and lesbian cohabiting couples: A 1-year follow-up study. *Journal of Social and Personal Relationships, 6,* 39-59.

Kurdek, L. (1991a). Correlates of relationship satisfaction in cohabiting gay and lesbian couples: Integration of contextual, investment, and problem-solving models. *Journal of Personality and Social Psychology, 61,* 910-922.

Kurdek, L. (1991b). The dissolution of gay and lesbian couples. *Journal of Social and Personal Relationships, 8,* 265-278.

Kurdek, L. (1993). The allocation of household labor in gay, lesbian, and heterosexual married couples. *Journal of Social Issues, 49*(3), 127-139.

Kurdek, L. (1995). Developmental changes in relationship quality in gay and lesbian cohabiting couples. *Developmental Psychology, 31,* 86-94.

Lancaster, J. B. (1989). Evolutionary and cross-cultural perspectives on single parenthood. In R. W. Bell & N. J. Bell (Eds.), *Sociobiology and the social sciences* (pp. 63-72). Lubbock: Texas Tech University Press.

Leaper, C., Carson, M., Baker, C., Holliday, H., & Myers, S. (1995). Self-disclosure and listener verbal support in same-gender and cross-gender friends' conversations. *Sex Roles, 33,* 387-404.

Leigh, B. C. (1989). Reasons for having and avoiding sex: Gender, sexual orientation, and relationship to sexual behavior. *Journal of Sex Research, 26,* 199-209.

Levenson, R. W., & Gottman, J. M. (1985). Physiological and affective predictors of change in relationship satisfaction. *Journal of Personality and Social Psychology, 49,* 85-94.

Maccoby, E. (1988). Gender as a social category. *Developmental Psychology, 24,* 755-765.

Maccoby, E. E. (1990). Gender and relationships: A developmental account. *American Psychologist, 45,* 513-520.

Maccoby, E. E., & Jacklin, C. N. (1987). Gender segregation in childhood. In H. W. Reese (Ed.), *Advances in child development and behavior* (Vol. 20, pp. 239-288). New York: Academic Press.

MacDermid, S. M., Huston, T. L., & McHale, S. M. (1990). Changes in marriage associated with the transition to parenthood: Individual differences as a function of sex-role attitudes and changes in the division of household labor. *Journal of Marriage and the Family, 52,* 475-486.

Major, B. (1993). Gender, entitlement, and the distribution of family labor. *Journal of Social Issues, 49*(3), 141-159.

Maltz, D. N., & Borker, R. A. (1983). A cultural approach to male-female miscommunication. In J. A. Gumperz (Ed.), *Language and social identity* (pp. 195-216). New York: Cambridge University Press.

Markman, H. J., Silvern, L., Clements, M., & Kraft-Hanak, S. (1993). Men and women dealing with conflict in heterosexual relationships. *Journal of Social Issues, 49*(3), 107-125.

Marshall, L. L. (1994). Physical and psychological abuse. In W. R. Cupach & B. H. Spitzberg (Eds.), *The dark side of interpersonal communication* (pp. 281-311). Hillsdale, NJ: Lawrence Erlbaum.

McCloskey, L. A., & Coleman, L. M. (1992). Differences without dominance: Children's talk in mixed and same-sex dyads. *Sex Roles, 27,* 241-258.

Michael, R. T., Gagnon, J. H., Laumann, E. O., & Kolata, G. (1994). *Sex in America: A definitive survey.* Boston, MA: Little, Brown.

Miller, J. B. (1991). Women's and men's scripts for interpersonal conflict. *Psychology of Women Quarterly, 15,* 15-29.

Moller, L. C., Hymel, S., & Rubin, K. H. (1992). Sex typing in play and popularity in middle childhood. *Sex Roles, 26,* 331-353.

Monsour, M. (1992). Meanings of intimacy in cross- and same-sex friendships. *Journal of Social and Personal Relationships, 9,* 277-295.

Monsour, M., Harris, B., & Kurtzweil, N. (1994). Challenges confronting cross-sex friendships: "Much ado about nothing?" *Sex Roles, 31,* 55-77.

Moore, M. M. (1985). Nonverbal courtship patterns in women: Context and consequences. *Ethology and Sociobiology, 6,* 237-247.

Muehlenhard, C. L., Goggins, M. F., Jones, J. M., & Satterfield, A. T. (1991). Sexual violence and coercion in close relationships. In K. McKinney & S. Sprecher (Eds.), *Sexuality in close relationships* (pp. 155-175). Hillsdale, NJ: Lawrence Erlbaum.

Muehlenhard, C. L., Julsonnet, S., Carlson, M. I., & Flarity-White, L. A. (1989). A cognitive-behavioral program for preventing sexual coercion. *The Behavior Therapist, 12,* 211-214.

Muehlenhard, C. L., & Linton, M. A. (1987). Date rape and sexual aggression in dating situations: Incidence and risk factors. *Journal of Counseling Psychology, 34,* 186-196.

Nardi, P. M. (1992). That's what friends are for: Friends as family in the gay and lesbian community. In K. Plummer (Ed.), *Modern homosexualities* (pp. 108-120). New York: Routledge.

Nardi, P. M., & Sherrod, D. (1994). Friendship in the lives of gay men and lesbians. *Journal of Social and Personal Relationships, 11,* 185-199.

Nevid, J. S. (1995). *Choices: Sex in the age of STDs.* Boston: Allyn & Bacon.

Noller, P., & White, A. (1990). The validity of the Communication Patterns Questionnaire. *Psychological Assessment: A Journal of Consulting and Clinical Psychology, 2,* 478-482.

Notarius, C. I., Benson, P. R., Sloane, D., Vanzetti, N., & Hornyak, L. M. (1989). Exploring the interface between perception and behavior: An analysis of marital interaction in distressed and nondistressed couples. *Behavioral Assessment, 11,* 39-64.

O'Connor, P. (1992). *Friendships between women: A critical review.* New York: Guilford.

O'Donahue, W., & Crouch, J. L. (1996). Marital therapy and gender-linked factors in communication. *Journal of Marital and Family Therapy, 22,* 87-101.

O'Meara, J. D. (1989). Cross-sex friendship: Four basic challenges of an ignored relationship. *Sex Roles, 21,* 525-543.

O'Meara, J. D. (1994). Cross-sex friendships opportunity challenge: Uncharted terrain for exploration. *Personal Relationship Issues, 2,* 4-7.

O'Sullivan, L. F., & Byers, E. S. (1992). College students' incorporation of initiator and restrictor roles in sexual dating interactions. *Journal of Sex Research, 29,* 435-446.

Parks, M., & Floyd, K. (1996). Meanings for closeness and intimacy in friendship. *Journal of Social and Personal Relationships, 13,* 85-107.

Peplau, L. A., & Gordon, S. L. (1985). Women and men in love: Gender differences in close heterosexual relationships. In V. E. O'Leary, R. K. Unger, & B. S. Wallston (Eds.), *Women, gender, and social psychology* (pp. 257-291). Hillsdale, NJ: Lawrence Erlbaum.

Peplau, L. A., Rubin, Z., & Hill, C. T. (1977). Sexual intimacy in dating relationships. *Journal of Social Issues, 33*(2), 86-109.

Perper, T., & Weis, D. L. (1987). Proceptive and rejective strategies of U.S. and Canadian college women. *Journal of Sex Research, 23,* 455-480.

Perry-Jenkins, M., & Folk, K. (1994). Class, couples, and conflict: Effects of the division of labor on assessments of marriage in dual-earner families. *Journal of Marriage and the Family, 56,* 165-180.

Philliber, W., & Hiller, D. (1979). A research note: Occupational attainments and perceptions of status among working wives. *Journal of Marriage and the Family, 41,* 59-62.

Pina, D. L., & Bengtson, V. L. (1993). The division of household labor and wives' happiness: Ideology, employment, and perceptions of support. *Journal of Marriage and the Family, 55,* 901-912.

Pleck, J. (1985). *Working wives, working husband.* Beverly Hills, CA: Sage.

Pleck, J. H., Sonenstein, F. L., & Ku, L. C. (1993a). Masculinity ideology and its correlates. In S. Oskamp & M. Costanzo (Eds.), *Gender issues in contemporary society* (pp. 85-110). Newbury Park, CA: Sage.

Pleck, J. H., Sonenstein, F. L., & Ku, L. C. (1993b). Masculinity ideology: Its impact on adolescent males' heterosexual relationships. *Journal of Social Issues, 49*(3), 11-29.

Rawlins, W. K. (1992). *Friendship matters: Communication, dialectics, and the life course.* Hawthorne, NY: Aldine de Gruyter.

Rawlins, W. K. (1994). Reflecting on (cross-sex) friendship: Describing the drama. *Personal Relationship Issues, 2*, 1-3.

Reid, H. M., & Fine, G. A. (1992). Self-disclosure in men's friendships: Variations associated with intimate relations. In P. M. Nardi (Ed.), *Men's friendships* (pp. 132-152). Newbury Park, CA: Sage.

Reis, H. T., Senchak, M., & Solomon, B. (1985). Sex differences in the intimacy of social interaction: Further examination of potential explanations. *Journal of Personality and Social Psychology, 5*, 1204-1217.

Renzetti, C. M. (1992). *Violent betrayal: Partner abuse in lesbian relationships.* Newbury Park, CA: Sage.

Risman, B. J. (1987). Intimate relationships from a microstructural perspective: Men who mother. *Gender and Society, 1*, 6-32.

Risman, B. J., & Schwartz, P. (1989). *Gender in intimate relationships: A microstructural approach.* Belmont, CA: Wadsworth.

Rivers, C. & Barnett, R. (1996). *She works/he works: How two-income families are happier, healthier, and better-off.* San Francisco, CA: Harper San Francisco.

Roese, N. H., Olson, J. M., Borenstein, M. N., Martin, A., & Shores, A. L. (1992). Same-sex touching behavior: The moderating role of homophobic attitudes. *Journal of Nonverbal Behavior, 16*, 249-259.

Rook, K. S., & Hammen, C. L. (1977). A cognitive perspective on the experience of sexual arousal. *Journal of Social Issues, 33*(2), 7-29.

Rose, S. M. (1984). How friendships end: Patterns among young adults. *Journal of Social and Personal Relationships, 1*, 267-277.

Rose, S. M. (1985). Same- and cross-sex friendships and the psychology of homosociality. *Sex Roles, 12*, 63-74.

Rose, S., & Frieze, I. H. (1993). Young singles' contemporary dating scripts. *Sex Roles, 28*, 499-509.

Rubin, J. Z., Provenzano, F. J., & Luria, Z. (1974). The eye of the beholder: Parents' views on sex of newborns. *American Journal of Orthopsychiatry, 44*, 512-519.

Rubin, L. (1975). *Just friends: The role of friendship in our lives.* New York: Harper & Row.

Rusbult, C. (1987). Responses to dissatisfaction in close relationships: The exit-voice-loyalty-neglect model. In D. Perlman & S. W. Duck (Eds.),

Intimate relationships: Development, dynamics, deterioration (pp. 209-238). London: Sage.

Sadalla, E. K., Kenrick, D. T., & Vershure, B. (1987). Dominance and heterosexual attraction. *Journal of Personality and Social Psychology, 52,* 730-738.

Sapadin, L. A. (1988). Friendship and gender: Perspectives of professional men and women. *Journal of Social and Personal Relationships,* 387-403.

Schwartz, P. (1995). *Love between equals: How peer marriages really work.* New York: Free Press.

Sedikides, C., Oliver, M. B., & Campbell, W. K. (1994). Perceived benefits and costs of romantic relationships for women and men: Implications for exchange theory. *Personal Relationships, 1,* 5-21.

Shotland, R. L., & Craig, J. M. (1988). Can men and women differentiate between friendly and sexually interested behavior. *Social Psychology Quarterly, 51,* 66-73.

Skrypnek, B. J., & Snyder, M. (1982). On the self-perpetuating nature of stereotypes about women and men. *Journal of Experimental Social Psychology, 18,* 277-291.

Snell, W. E., Belk, S. S., Flowers, A., & Warren, J. (1988). Women's and men's willingness to self-disclose to therapists and friends: The moderating influence of instrumental, expressive, masculine, and feminine topics. *Sex Roles, 18,* 769-776.

Sprague, J., & Quadagno, D. (1989). Gender and sexual motivation: An exploration of two assumptions. *Journal of Psychology and Human Sexuality, 2,* 57-76.

Sprecher, S. (1989). Premarital sexual standards for different categories of individuals. *Journal of Sex Research, 26,* 232-248.

Sprecher, S., McKinney, K., & Orbuch, T. L. (1987). Has the double standard disappeared? An experimental test. *Social Psychology Quarterly, 50,* 24-31.

Stafford, L., & Canary, D. J. (1991). Maintenance strategies and romantic relationship type, gender, and relational characteristics. *Journal of Social and Personal Relationships, 8,* 217-242.

Steil, J. M. (1994). Equality and entitlement in marriage: Benefits and barriers. In M. J. Lerner & G. Mikula (Eds.), *Entitlement and the affectional bond: Justice in close relationships* (pp. 229-258). New York: Plenum.

Steil, J. M., & Turetsky, B. A. (1987). Is equal better? The relationship between marital equality and psychological symptomatology. In S. Oskamp (Ed.), *Family processes and problems: Social psychological aspects* (pp. 73-95). Newbury Park, CA: Sage.

Steil, J. M., & Weltman, K. (1990). Marital inequality: The importance of resources, personal attributes, and social norms on career valuing and the allocation of domestic responsibilities. *Sex Roles, 24,* 161-179.

Stets, J. E., & Straus, M. A. (1990a). Gender differences in reporting marital violence and its medical and psychological consequences. In M. A. Straus & R. J. Gelles (Eds.), *Physical violence in American families: Risk factors and adaptations to violence in 8,145 families* (pp. 151-165). New Brunswick, NJ: Transaction.

Stets, J. E., & Straus, M. A. (1990b). The marriage license as a hitting license: A comparison of assaults in dating, cohabiting, and married couples. In M. A. Straus & R. J. Gelles (Eds.), *Physical violence in American families: Risk factors and adaptations to violence in 8,145 families* (pp. 227-244). New Brunswick, NJ: Transaction.

Stevens, G., Owens, D., & Schaefer, E. C. (1990). Education and attractiveness in marriage choice. *Social Psychology Quarterly, 53*, 62-70.

Straus, M. A. (1990). Measuring intrafamily conflict and violence: The Conflict Tactics (CT) Scales. In M. A. Straus & R. J. Gelles (Eds.), *Physical violence in American families: Risk factors and adaptations to violence in 8,145 families* (pp. 29-47). New Brunswick, NJ: Transaction.

Straus, M. A., & Gelles, R. J. (1990a). How violent are American families? Estimates from the National Family Violence Resurvey and other studies. In M. A. Straus & R. J. Gelles (Eds.), *Physical violence in American families: Risk factors and adaptations to violence in 8,145 families* (pp. 95-112). New Brunswick, NJ: Transaction.

Straus, M. A., & Gelles, R. J. (1990b). *Physical violence in American families: Risk factors and adaptations to violence in 8,145 families.* New Brunswick, NJ: Transaction Publishers.

Swain, S. O. (1992). Men's friendships with women: Intimacy, sexual boundaries, and the informant role. In P. M. Nardi (Ed.), *Men's friendships* (pp. 153-171). Newbury Park, CA: Sage.

Tannen, D. (1990). Gender differences in topical coherence: Creating involvement in best friends' talk. *Discourse Processes, 13*, 73-90.

Thompson, L. (1991). Family work: Women's sense of fairness. *Journal of Family Issues, 12*, 181-196.

Thorne, B. (1986). Girls and boys together . . . but mostly apart: Gender arrangements in elementary schools. In W. W. Hartup & Z. Rubin (Eds.), *Relationships and development* (pp. 167-184). Hillsdale, NJ: Lawrence Erlbaum.

Thorne, B., & Luria, Z. (1986). Sexuality and gender in children's daily worlds. *Social Problems, 33*, 176-190.

Trent, K., & South, S. (1989). Structural determinants of the divorce rate: A cross-societal analysis. *Journal of Marriage and the Family, 51*, 391-404.

Trivers, R. L. (1972). Parental investment and sexual selection. In B. Campbell (Ed.), *Sexual selection and the descent of man: 1871-1971* (pp. 136-179). Chicago, IL: Aldine.

Unger, R., & Crawford, M. (1996). *Women and gender: A feminist psychology.* New York: McGraw-Hill.

U.S. Bureau of Labor. (1994). *1993 handbook on women workers: Trends and issues.* Washington, DC: Government Printing Office.

Vannoy-Hiller, D., & Philliber, W. W. (1989). *Equal partners: Successful women in marriage.* Newbury Park, CA: Sage.

Warr, P., & Parry, G. (1982). Paid employment and women's psychological well-being. *Psychological Bulletin, 91,* 498-516.

Weiss, L., & Lowenthal, M. F. (1975). Life course perspectives on friendship. In M. F. Lowenthal, M. Turner, D. Chiriboga, & Associates (Eds.), *Four stages of life* (pp. 48-61). San Francisco: Jossey-Bass.

Wells Guttau, L. (1996). *Causal models of work-family conflict from family and organizational perspectives.* Unpublished doctoral dissertation, Old Dominion University.

Werking, K. J. (1994). Hidden assumptions: A critique of existing cross-sex friendship research. *Personal Relationships Issues, 2,* 8-11.

Weston, K. (1991). *Families we choose: Gays, lesbians, and kinship.* New York: Columbia University.

Wheeler, L., Reis, H. T., & Bond, M. H. (1989). Collectivism-individualism in everyday social life: The middle kingdom and the melting pot. *Journal of Personality and Social Psychology, 57,* 79-86.

White, J. W., & Koss, M. P. (1991). Courtship violence: Incidence in a national sample of higher education students. *Violence and Victims, 6,* 247-256.

White, L. K., Booth, A., & Edwards, J. N. (1986). Children and marital happiness: Why the negative correlation? *Journal of Family Issues, 6,* 435-450.

Whiting, B. B., & Edwards, C. P. (1988). *Children of different worlds.* Cambridge, MA: Harvard University Press.

Williams, S. S., Kimble, D. L., Covell, N. H., Weiss, L. H., Newton, K. J., Fisher, J. D., & Fisher, W. A. (1992). College students use implicit personality theory instead of safer sex. *Journal of Applied Social Psychology, 22,* 921-933.

Winstead, B. A. (1986). Sex differences in same-sex friendships. In V. J. Derlega & B. A. Winstead (Eds.), *Friendship and social interaction* (pp. 81-99). New York, NY: Springer-Verlag.

Winstead, B. A., Derlega, V. J., Montgomery, M. J., & Pilkington, C. (1995). The quality of friendships at work and job satisfaction. *Journal of Social and Personal Relationships, 12,* 199-216.

Wood, J., & Inman, C. C. (1993). In a different mode: Masculine styles of communicating closeness. *Journal of Applied Communication Research, 21,* 279-295.

Wright, P. H. (1988). Interpreting research on gender differences in friendship: A case for moderation and a plea for caution. *Journal of Social and Personal Relationships, 5,* 367-373.

Wright, P. H., & Scanlon, M. B. (1991). Gender role orientations and friendship: Some attenuation, but gender differences abound. *Sex Roles, 24,* 551-566.

Yllo, K. A., & Straus, M. A. (1990). Patriarchy and violence against wives: The impact of structural and normative factors. In M. A. Straus & R. J. Gelles (Eds.), *Physical violence in American families: Risk factors and adaptations to violence in 8,145 families* (pp. 383-399). New Brunswick, NJ: Transaction Publishers.

Zook, K. B. (1996, February 11). Of love and madness: Why women stay when the perfect mate turns abusive. *The Washington Post,* p. C5.

Index

About the Authors

Valerian J. Derlega, Ph.D., is Professor of Psychology at Old Dominion University, Norfolk, Virginia. He received his doctoral degree in social psychology from the University of Maryland in 1971. His research interests include self-disclosure and privacy regulation in close relationships, social support and coping with stress, the impact of the male role on relationships, and therapy as a personal relationship. He is also conducting research on social aspects of coping with the HIV infection. He is on the Editorial Boards of the *Journal of Social and Personal Relationships, Personal Relationships, Journal of Social and Clinical Psychology,* and the *Journal of Gender, Culture, and Health.*

Suzanna Rose, Ph.D., is Professor of Psychology in the Institute for Women's and Gender Studies at the University of Missouri-St.

Louis. She received her doctorate in 1979 from the University of Pittsburgh, where she began her research on friendship. Her current interests focus on how gender, sexual orientation, and race influence friendship, courtship, and close relationships. She also does research on hate-crime victimization and runs a hotline to aid lesbian and gay survivors of violence.

Barbara A. Winstead, Ph.D., is Professor of Psychology at Old Dominion University and Graduate Program Director of the Psy.D. program of the Virginia Consortium. She received her doctoral degree in personality and developmental psychology from Harvard University in 1980. A licensed clinical psychologist, she has taught undergraduate and graduate courses in gender and relationships, psychology of women, theories of personality, and research methods. She has conducted research on gender and social support, friendships, dating relationships, and abuse in relationships. She is an Advisory Editor for *Contemporary Psychology.* She is currently creating measures to assess styles of managing multiple life roles.